Literary Feast

◆

The Famous Authors Cookbook

Vol. I, 2009

King County
Library System Foundation

with foreword by Greg Atkinson

Compiled and Edited by
Terry J. LaBrue, A.P.R.

CLASSIC DAY
PUBLISHING

Seattle, Washington
Portland, Oregon
Denver, Colorado
Vancouver, B.C.
Scottsdale, Arizona
Minneapolis, Minnesota

Classic Day Publishing
2925 Fairview Avenue East
Seattle, Washington 98102
877-728-8837
info@classicdaypub.com

Contents

Set the Table.

Authors and books, food and cooks, readers and libraries. These are all winning combinations with far-reaching possibilities. Combine the rich ingredients, stir with vigor, and *voilá* you have a *Literary Feast*.

The King County Library System Foundation presents this exciting new cookbook to benefit vital literacy and lifelong learning programs in our community. King County, Washington, is one of the most highly educated and technologically advanced areas of our country and our library system is the second busiest in the United States. Yet, there are thousands of children and families in our community who lack the educational resources to read a menu, succeed in school, operate a computer or find a better job.

Each year, more than 120,000 children and adults benefit from Foundation-supported programs. Proceeds from this fascinating compendium of recipes will enable the Foundation to sustain and expand its support for innovative programs that build early literacy skills, provide reading incentives for youth and offer lifelong learning activities for adults.

Creative and dedicated people contributed to this project and we offer hearty applause to all. Special appreciation goes to many dedicated individuals who toiled for more than two years to make this cookbook a reality.

- To Elliott Wolf, Classic Day Publishing, for conceiving the vision and for his enthusiasm and encouragement.

- To Terry LaBrue, LaBrue Communications, for his dedication to libraries and for his talents in writing, editing and managing the project resulting in a unique and appetizing publication. Kudos to Katie Young who ably assisted this process.

- To Angelina Benedetti, Collection Management Services, and J Tarner, Graphics, at King County Library System for their support and efforts in contacting authors and securing photographs. Special applause to Claire Wilkinson, KCLS Foundation, for her participation in and contributions to this project.

- To King County Library System Director Bill Ptacek and the KCLS Board of Trustees for seeking innovative ways to promote and encourage literacy and lifelong learning in our libraries and in our community.

- To the King County Library System Foundation Board of Directors for their passionate support of libraries and for their continuing endorsement of this project.

- To the authors' agents and publicists for engaging their clients and encouraging participation in this cookbook.

- To chef and author Greg Atkinson for capturing the essence of this unique project and recipe collection in his foreword.

- And, special appreciation to the authors who enrich our lives with their words and who so generously shared their favorite recipes and personal stories.

The King County Library System Foundation wishes you a feast of great books and memorable meals to savor. *Bon appetit.*

Jeanne Thorsen
Executive Director
King County Library System Foundation

It is no more necessary that a man should remember the different dinners and suppers, which have made him healthy, than the different books that have made him wise. Let us see the results of good food in a strong body, and the results of great reading in a full and powerful mind.

– Sydney Smith, English
Essayist, 1771-1845

The King County Library System Foundation

The King County Library System Foundation creates opportunities to bring literacy, learning, and library access to all members of our community. The Foundation provides the venture capital for library initiatives that address community needs, the funding for value-added programs and resources plus the vision to ensure that our public library system is vibrant, relevant, and central to our lives.

As our community grows and changes and as sources of information rapidly multiply, providing easy access to information, without charge, for all members of our community becomes ever more challenging. Yet providing such access is necessary to ensure that everyone has the literacy and learning opportunities to share in the quality of life so many of us enjoy.

The King County Library System strives to be agile and innovative in providing services while offering relevance to residents who represent an array of ages, ethnicities, cultures, languages, and interests. The Foundation extends the Library System's ability to meet the needs of our communities. Here is a snapshot of Foundation-supported programs:

ENCOURAGING LIFELONG READERS

Our vision is that all children in our community will be ready to read by their first day of school. Research shows that children prepare to read as early as infancy and reading to – and with – young children is one of the most effective ways parents can support brain development and early-learning skills.

- The *Ready to Read* program and *Fiestas de Alfabetización Temprana en Español* bring early literacy training to parents and caregivers. The *Ready to Read* and *Listo para Leer* guidebooks feature stories, wordplays, and songs to encourage parent and child reading activities.
- *Books for Babies* brings books and tips for reading together to low-income parents of newborns.
- The *Summer Reading Program for Preschoolers* involves pre-readers and their parents in this popular activity.

PROMOTING READING AND THE PURSUIT OF KNOWLEDGE

The Foundation supports programs that motivate the enjoyment of reading, the improvement of comprehension skills, and the pursuit of knowledge, whether for practical purposes or for its own sake.

- *The Summer Reading Program* includes activities for elementary school age students.
- The *Read 3, Get 1 Free* program for teens involves writing book reviews and opportunities to film reviews and trailers in the *Read. Flip. Win.* contest.
- *The Global Reading Challenge* involves more than 200 fourth- and fifth-grade teams in a friendly and spirited 'battle of the books' competition.
- *Ready, Set, Read!* challenges students in the early grades to establish the reading habit.
- The Foundation also supports free SAT preparation classes and one-to-one tutoring in *Study Zones*.

ENHANCING LIBRARY ACCESS

Reaching out to the community with invitations to visit the library and use its resources is vital. For many people, a new program presents an opportunity to experience the public library for the first time.

- Attracting teens, especially boys, to the library is an important goal, and the *Game On!* program brings in new and returning youth to local libraries.
- *The Big Read is* a community-wide reading program that involves popular classics.
- The KCLS Foundation sees significant value in building a new generation of librarians who will serve our community and awards scholarships to KCLS staff members seeking their masters' degrees in library and information science.
- Reconnecting readers of all ages with books is a new initiative designed to promote the discovery of new authors, stories, topics, and ideas.

CELEBRATING AUTHORS AND THE JOY OF READING

The Foundation's annual Literary Lions Gala celebrates the talents of prominent local authors and the joy of reading. More than 300 guests attend the gala each year, which showcases 30 popular authors from the Pacific Northwest.

LOOKING TO THE FUTURE

The Foundation's vision is for a community of avid readers and eager learners served by a public library system offering abundant learning opportunities for everyone. This future involves:

- A community of lifelong learners that turns to and relies on the public library for inspiration and information.
- A library that overflows with intellectual adventures, innovative programs, and incredibly easy access to information.
- A library that is a vibrant and relevant component of our community.

Libraries provide abundant resources for our families, friends, colleagues, and neighbors as well as information to launch new ideas and transform lives. The King County Library System Foundation is making our ambitious vision a reality for everyone, and creating a community of readers.

For more information, visit www.kcls.org (King County Library System) and www.kclsfoundation.org (KCLS Foundation).

King County
Library System
Foundation

960 Newport Way NW
Issaquah, WA 98027
425.369.3448

Foreword

Sometimes people say I am unusual because I cook and I write. I smile and nod and think aren't these things that everyone should do? I cook and write for one reason; I like to make stuff. I'm not very good with power tools or I would make houses and furniture. But I can handle a pen and a whisk, so I make cakes and books. I think it's some basic human need. Ask any elementary school teacher. Kids love to make stuff. Sometimes things don't turn out the way we think they should – but we keep trying because that's just what people do. What I like most is eating something so good that it makes me want to cook or reading something so good that it makes me want to write.

Sometimes in fact, I evaluate the quality of what I am reading by gauging how motivated I am to write when I finish the book. If I don't even think about writing when I'm done reading, then I will probably never think about that book again. If I feel compelled to rush to the computer and write something right away, I liked the book a lot. If the book is very, very good, I go glum, wishing I could write half as well as the author does. Then, for days, I will not write a thing because I feel unworthy of putting words together at all.

Most of the recipes in this book are new to me. But many of them will be familiar soon enough. I'm going to make Rick Steve's "Cowboy Cookies" right now, because they're Rick Steve's and they're cowboy cookies. I'm going to make Kaya McLaren's "Kaya's Cookies" too – just because they're cookies.

Susan Wiggs is my neighbor on Bainbridge Island and I am a heel because I have never read her prize-winning novels. But I *will* make her "Rosemary Olive Oil Cake" because my garden is teeming with rosemary and I love olive oil. Next time we meet, I can wax poetic about her cake so we won't have to talk about her books. It will be perfect. The recipe calls for a Bundt pan and I have one of those hanging on my kitchen wall, crying out for a worthy recipe. Since the recipe calls for a quarter-cup of Grand Marnier, I'll have an excuse to stock my pantry with a bottle that I can tap into when I finally settle in some winter afternoon and actually read one of Susan's books.

I will make Karin Slaughter's recipe for "Cathy's Coke Roast" because I share her Southern heritage. Before I came to the Northwest, I spent a sultry childhood on the Gulf Coast of Florida. Like Slaughter, I am "interested in sex, violence, religion and all the things that make life interesting." Besides, I love braised meats. The chemistry of marinating a roast in sweet, acidic, and slightly bitter Coca Cola just makes sense to me. But I am going to tweak her recipe. I refuse to throw away the coke after marinating the meat; I'm going to leave it in and let it have its wicked way with the beef while it simmers.

The conundrum of Bharti Kirchner's "Thai Tortellini" is so compelling that I will have to make it just to see if it makes any sense at all. I know it will, because I spent a weekend with Kirchner at a writer's retreat on Whidbey Island. I know that everything she does makes sense, even when it utterly defies convention. And I'm going to serve Pepper Schwartz's "Thanksgiving Wild Rice" this Thanksgiving because that holiday really needs sexing up – it's way too puritanical. When I present the rice, chock full of nuts and dried fruit, I'll say it's Pepper Schwartz's recipe. That statement alone will give us all a chance to talk about sex instead of all that boring stuff we're supposed to be thankful for.

Of course I'll make Alice Water's "Fresh-Pickled Vegetables" from *The Art of Simple Food* because I just love her. She is the James Beard of our generation, the voice of reason in a food world gone mad. And, her palate is impeccable. Besides, I need something to do with extra vegetables when I come home from the farmer's market with more than I can reasonably use.

Best of all, I'm going to take this book out of the kitchen and bring it to bed with me. I'll read every word and think about all the wonderful things I'm going to cook and all the wonderful things I'm going to write. Then, I will sleep and dream and wake up refreshed and ready to read and write and cook some more.

– Greg Atkinson

Literary Feast

◆

The Famous
Authors Cookbook

Arthur Agatston, M.D.

A preventive cardiologist and associate professor of medicine at the University of Miami, Dr. Arthur Agatston has taken the publishing world by storm. He has authored numerous scientific articles and is frequently quoted in the media as an expert on diet and heart-disease prevention. Combined sales of his mega-bestseller, *The South Beach Diet*, and companion titles, including the recently published *The South Beach Diet Supercharged,* have topped 22 million copies. Agatston maintains a private practice as a partner at South Florida Cardiology Associates and lives in Miami Beach with his wife and two sons.

ABOUT THE RECIPE:

"This recipe is one of the delicious new recipes created for *The South Beach Diet Supercharged,* the new bestseller. Deceptively simple, this tasty chicken dish can be enjoyed on any phase of the diet. It works just as well for company as it does on a busy weeknight. Make extra for lunch or dinner the next day: Thinly slice the chicken and serve it over simply dressed salad greens or roughly chop the chicken and toss it with fresh spinach, a little olive oil and warm whole-wheat pasta. You'll enjoy it."

– Dr. Agatston

Sun-Dried Tomato and Feta–Stuffed Chicken Breasts

1/3 cup reduced-fat feta cheese
2 sun-dried tomatoes (from a jar), finely chopped
1 garlic clove, minced
1/2 teaspoon dried basil
Freshly ground black pepper
4 (6-oz.) boneless, skinless chicken breasts
Salt
2 teaspoons extra-virgin olive oil

Heat the oven to 425 degrees.

In a small bowl, combine cheese, tomatoes, garlic, and basil. Season with pepper and mash together well with a fork.

Butterfly chicken by carefully slicing horizontally along the long edge of each breast, three-quarters of the way through. Open up each breast and spread inside with one-fourth of the feta mixture.

Close breast over filling and press edges together to seal. Season lightly with salt and pepper. In a large ovenproof skillet, heat oil over medium-high heat. Add chicken and cook until browned on both sides, about 2 minutes per side. Transfer skillet to oven and bake until chicken is cooked through, about 20-25 minutes. Remove from oven and serve warm.

Nutrition at a Glance: Per serving: 232 calories, 6 g fat, 2 g saturated fat, 42 g protein, 1 g carbohydrate, 0 g fiber, 326 mg sodium

Makes 4 servings

Elaine Ambrose

Elaine Ambrose is the author of 100 magazine articles and five books. Her humorous book for women golfers, titled *The Red Tease – A Woman's Adventures in Golf,* won the Bronze Award for Humor in a national competition sponsored by Foreword Magazine. Her children's book, *Gators & Taters,* received an award as Best New Children's Book of 2003 and was one of only 50 books selected for Bowker's National Reading List. Her second children's book, *The Magic Potato,* was adopted by the Idaho State Board of Education for inclusion in the statewide school curriculum. Elaine's humorous new book, *Menopause Sucks!,* was released in the summer of 2008.

Elaine's first national publication came at the ripe old age of eleven. She graduated with Phi Beta Kappa scholastic honors from the University of Idaho with a degree in journalism and became Idaho's first female television news reporter and talk show hostess. She currently owns Mill Park Publishing in Eagle, Idaho, and is a popular humorous speaker throughout the country.

ABOUT THE RECIPE:

"Growing up on an isolated potato farm in southern Idaho provided me with plenty of time to imagine tall tales and sassy stories. I conjured up ideas while I worked in the fields, weeding potatoes and hoeing beets. Fall was an arduous but crucial time on the farm. We got out of school for two weeks every October to work in the fields, and the potato harvest continued day and night until the work was done. I worked in a potato harvester, which was a dirty, noisy job to pick out rocks and vines as the potatoes moved along the chain to the truck. Each evening when we came home for a break, my mother would always have a big pot of potato and sausage soup on the stove. A bowl of this hearty soup and some homemade bread would sustain us for several hours after we returned to the fields. I no longer have to work the harvest, but I continue to make and savor this delicious soup."

– Elaine Ambrose

Ambrose Potato Sausage Soup

1 lb. bulk sausage
1 cup chopped onion
1 cup chopped celery
4-6 large Idaho russet potatoes, peeled and cubed
1 Tbsp. mustard seeds
2 tsp. salt
1 cup light cream
3 cups whole milk
2 cups mild Cheddar cheese
Optional: 2 cans (10 oz.) any flavor cream soup
Chopped parsley for garnish

Brown the sausage in a large skillet over low heat until crisp. Remove the meat to a warm plate with a slotted spoon. Drain the drippings and reserve one tablespoon of drippings. Add the onion and celery to the drippings and sauté until tender. Add the potatoes, mustard seeds, and salt. Add just enough water to cover the potatoes. Simmer for 15 minutes or until the potatoes are tender but still firm.

Reduce heat and stir in the cream and milk. Add the canned soup if a thicker soup is desired. Heat thoroughly but don't boil. Pour into large mugs and garnish with parsley. Add homemade bread or corn bread, an apple salad, gingerbread cookies, and some warm cider for a fabulous fall feast.

Yield: 8 servings

Susan Andersen

Susan Andersen writes contemporary romance with a touch of suspense and comedy to keep things interesting. Her books have spent many weeks on the *USA Today* and *New York Times* extended bestseller lists. She is the proud mother of a grown son and a native of the Pacific Northwest, where she lives with her husband and "The Boys" – her cats Boo and Mojo.

PUBLISHED WORKS:

Cutting Loose, Coming Undone, Just for Kicks, Skintight, Hot & Bothered, Getting Lucky, Head Over Heels, All Shook Up, Baby, I'm Yours, Be My Baby, Baby, Don't Go, Obsessed, Present Danger, Exposure, On Thin Ice and *Shadow Dance.*

ABOUT THE RECIPE:

"I love to cross-country ski, both classic and skate, so I spend hours in the frigid weather. And nothing warms you up after a long day on the trails like a hot bowl of soup. This is one of my all-time faves."

– *Susan Anderson*

Tortellini Soup

½ cup finely chopped onion
½ cup finely chopped celery
½ cup finely chopped green bell pepper
2 cloves garlic, minced
2 Tbsp. olive oil
2 Tbsp. all-purpose flour
2 cans vegetable or chicken broth
15 oz. (1 can) tomato sauce
14.5 oz. (1 can) diced tomatoes
1 cup tortellini, cooked
½ tsp. each oregano, basil, sage, pepper and sugar
2 tsp. parsley

Sauté the first four ingredients in a little olive oil until soft. Add the flour and stir. Slowly add vegetable or chicken broth, stirring constantly; bring to a boil. Add remaining ingredients and simmer for 15 minutes.

Serves 4 hungry skiers

Kelley Armstrong

Kelley Armstrong is the author of *The New York Times* bestselling *Otherworld* paranormal suspense series. Armstrong grew up in Ontario, Canada, where she still lives with her family. A former computer programmer, she's now escaped her corporate cubicle and hopes never to return. Her website is www.KelleyArmstrong.com.

PUBLISHED WORKS:

Women of the Otherworld series and *The Summoning*

ABOUT THE RECIPE:

"There's a running gag in my books about pancakes. But personally, I prefer French toast. This is a recipe I pull out for every Christmas brunch. It's much easier than cooking up individual slices...and it's much more popular! It can also be made the night before and refrigerated."

– Kelley Armstrong

Stuffed French Toast
(Adapted from *Cooking Light*, Dec. 2001)

18-20 slices of multigrain bread
2 cups low fat milk
1¼ cups egg substitute, divided
¾ cups sugar, divided
2 tsp. vanilla extract
⅛ tsp. ground nutmeg
2 8-oz. blocks of cream cheese
½ tsp. cinnamon
Maple syrup (optional)

1. Preheat oven to 350 degrees. Coat a 13"x 9" baking dish with cooking spray.

2. Trim crusts from bread. Spread half of bread in baking dish.

3. Combine milk, ¾ cup egg substitute and ¼ cup sugar in a bowl. Stir with a whisk. Pour half of mixture over bread in dish.

4. Combine ½ cup egg substitute, ½ cup sugar, vanilla, nutmeg and cream cheese in mixer. Beat until smooth. Pour over moist bread in dish.

5. Top with remaining bread and pour remaining milk mixture over top.

6. Sprinkle with cinnamon.

7. Bake for 50 minutes.

8. Let cool 5-10 minutes before cutting and serving. Serve with optional maple syrup.

Serves 10-12

Greg Atkinson

Director of Culinary Consulting, a menu and recipe development company, Greg Atkinson cooks, writes, and speaks in venues ranging from professional kitchens to university lecture halls. His latest book, *West Coast Cooking*, explores the personalities and ingredients that shaped America's most influential regional cuisine. A contributing editor to *Food Arts* magazine and *The Seattle Times*, he can be heard weekly on Seattle's NPR affiliate KUOW, 94.9 FM.

Atkinson was awarded The M.F.K. Fisher Distinguished Writing Award from the James Beard Foundation in 2001. He is a Certified Culinary Professional with the International Association of Culinary Professionals and has served on the board of directors for Chef's Collaborative and Slow Food Seattle.

ABOUT THE RECIPE:

"My mother's kitchen table was a five-foot round Victorian relic surrounded by eight old wooden office chairs; we called them the Perry Mason chairs because they looked exactly like the chairs on the old television show. Night after night for decades on end, she filled the table with delectable meals cooked from scratch following formulas inherited from her mother. These formulas could not really be called recipes because not only were they not written down; they were not even really talked about. Almost everything was braised. Pot roast got seared in oil, then bathed in leftover coffee, beef bouillon, black pepper and dried onions for a slow simmer that rendered it fork tender. In the broth surrounding the roast, she would cook noodles so that they absorbed the flavor of the roast. Chicken was summarily dispatched in almost the same way with chicken broth as the braising liquid and rice instead of noodles to absorb the juices. It may be thought of as comfort food, but for me recreating these old dishes is electrifying. I am transported not to some idyllic place from childhood, but launched fully into the present with heightened senses and a grand sense of having come from one place and arrived in another with this powerful culinary connection between the two."

– Greg Atkinson

Chicken with Rice

1 3$\frac{1}{2}$ to 4-pound free-range (preferably organic) chicken
   or 6 boneless chicken thighs
1 Tbsp. Kosher salt
1 tsp. freshly ground black pepper
$\frac{1}{4}$ cup olive oil
1 medium onion, peeled and thinly sliced
2 cups long-grain white rice such as jasmine or Basmati
4 cloves garlic, peeled and chopped
1 Bay leaf
1 tsp. dried thyme leaves
2 cups white wine
2 cups organic chicken broth

If using a whole chicken, cut it into eight pieces. Sprinkle the pieces or the boneless thighs with salt and pepper. In a Dutch oven, brown the chicken pieces in the oil, turning several times.

Pull the chicken out of the pan and in the oil, sauté the onion until it is soft and slightly browned. Stir in the rice, garlic, bay leaf and thyme, then pour in white wine and chicken broth and bring the liquid to a boil.

Put the chicken pieces back in the pot, reduce heat to low, and cover. Simmer until the rice has absorbed the cooking liquid and the chicken is cooked through, about 35 minutes.

Serve the chicken hot with rice and carrots.

Kit Bakke

Kit Bakke, a Seattle native and 1960's activist with the Weather Underground, became a mother, a wife, a pediatric nurse and a business consultant before turning to Louisa May Alcott for advice about living the rest of her life. In her book, *Miss Alcott's E-Mail,* the two women's letters cross the centuries to show us a Louisa who was no "little woman" and provide a story which *The Washington Post* says reads "like a wonderful movie shot with a hand-held camera." *Library Journal* notes "Bakke draws stimulating parallels between Alcott's life in the 1860s and her own background as a nurse and 1960s antiwar activist. Through Alcott, Bakke explores such issues as feminism, war, transcendentalism, nursing the sick, writing and civil rights."

PUBLISHED WORKS:

Miss Alcott's E-Mail and *Yours for Reforms of All Kinds.*

ABOUT THE RECIPE:

"Louisa May Alcott's family members were supporters of Dr. Sylvester Graham, who was a mid-19th century proponent of exercise, natural foods and homeopathic medicine. He invented the Graham cracker in 1829. Crackers were made from unbolted wheat, which is now known as Graham flour. Here is a recipe for real Graham crackers from my book, *Miss Alcott's E-mail.* It is well worth making and will put you off grocery store graham crackers forever after."

— *Kit Bakke*

Real Graham Crackers

$^{1}/_{2}$ cup butter
$^{2}/_{3}$ cup brown sugar
2 cups Graham flour
$^{1}/_{2}$ tsp. salt
$^{1}/_{2}$ tsp. baking powder
$^{1}/_{4}$ tsp. cinnamon
$^{1}/_{4}$ cup water

Mix butter and brown sugar. Add graham flour, salt, baking powder and cinnamon. Add water.

Work well with hands (or, if you don't mind being historically inaccurate, use your mixer), then let sit for about 30 minutes, or up to overnight, in the fridge.

Roll out on floured board to $^{1}/_{8}$-inch thickness. Cut into squares or rounds and prick all over with a fork. Bake on greased sheet pan in 350-degree oven for about 12 minutes.

David Baldacci

David Baldacci was born in Virginia, in 1960, where he currently resides. He received a Bachelor of Arts in political science from Virginia Commonwealth University and a law degree from the University of Virginia. He practiced law for nine years in Washington, D.C., as both a trial and corporate attorney.

David Baldacci has published 17 novels: *Absolute Power, Total Control, The Winner, The Simple Truth, Saving Faith, Wish You Well, Last Man Standing, The Christmas Train, Split Second, Hour Game, The Camel Club, The Collectors, Simple Genius, Stone Cold,* and *The Whole Truth*; and in his young adult series, *Freddy and the French Fries: Fries Alive!* and *Freddy and the French Fries: The Adventures of Silas Finklebean.*

His works have been in numerous worldwide magazines, newspapers, journals, and publications. He has authored seven original screenplays. His books have been translated into more than 40 languages and sold in more than 80 countries.

ABOUT THE RECIPE:

"This recipe is one that my Italian grandmother, Angelina Ceechini Baldacci, taught my mother (a non-Italian) to make for my father. We were all the fortunate recipients of that cooking lesson. After my mother went back to work, my father took on some of the cooking duties and I remember on Saturday mornings after I'd finished my paper route, helping him in the kitchen by turning the manual meat grinder while we made the sauce for the eggplant and other recipes. As good as it was, nothing we ever did came close to my grandmother's original work. Enjoy."

– David Baldacci

Eggplant Parmigiana
(A Baldacci Family Recipe)

4 Tbsp. olive oil
1 garlic clove, minced
1 large onion, chopped
2 16-oz. cans of tomatoes
2 tsp. sugar
½ tsp. oregano leaves
½ tsp. basil
½ tsp. salt
1 cup dried breadcrumbs
2 eggs
2 Tbsp. water
1 large eggplant (cut into ½ inch slices)
½ cup grated Parmesan cheese
18 oz. package mozzarella cheese cut into ¼ inch slices

1. In a 9-inch skillet over medium, heat 2 Tbsp. olive oil, cook garlic and onion until tender. Add the next five ingredients, reduce heat and cook covered for 30 minutes.
2. On waxed paper, place breadcrumbs, in a small dish beat the eggs and water together with a fork. Dip eggplant slices in the egg mixture then in the breadcrumbs, repeat to coat twice.
3. Grease 13"x 9" baking dish. In a 12-inch skillet over medium, heat 2 Tbsp. olive oil and cook a few eggplant slices at a time until golden brown. Add more oil as needed.
4. Preheat oven to 350 degrees. Arrange half of the eggplant slices in the baking dish, cover with half of the tomato mixture, sprinkle with half of the Parmesan cheese and top with half mozzarella cheese. Repeat layers with the final layer being mozzarella cheese. Bake for 25 minutes.

Serves 4 - 6

Greg Bear

Greg Bear is the author of more than 30 books of science fiction and fantasy, including *Blood Music, The Forge of God, Darwin's Radio,* and *Quantico.* He is married to Astrid Andersen Bear and is the father of Erik and Alexandra. Awarded two Hugos and five Nebulas for his fiction (one of only two authors to win a Nebula in every category), Bear has been called the "Best working writer of hard science fiction" by the *Ultimate Encyclopedia of Science Fiction.* His most recent novel is *Quantico,* a near-future examination of law enforcement, politics, and terror both domestic and religious. *Darwin's Radio* and *Darwin's Children* form a sequence about viruses and human evolution. He can be reached through his website: www.gregbear.com.

ABOUT THE RECIPE:

"Every year, in July, my wife and I hold a party to celebrate the Clarion West writers workshop – a six-week affair that allows beginning writers (or writers who want more familiarity with science fiction or fantasy) to spend days under the tutelage of six professionals in those fields. The workshop has been remarkably successful over the years – and a great deal of fun.

The party is held at our lakefront house, and Astrid usually serves a mouth-watering chicken mole to accompany many salads and desserts brought in by guests.

One of my favorite incidents occurred over 15 years ago. A young writer had joined me at the end of the dock to dabble our feet over the water and talk theory. After a few minutes, she asked, "What's the *real* secret to writing and getting published?"

'Well,' I began. 'To tell the truth, it's…'

At that point, the four-year-old daughter of some dear friends pushed herself between us and said, 'I know the Lithuanian word for tree!'

Obviously this was a coded message from the secret muses.

The young writer never did learn the secret, which has been kept safe ever since."

– Greg Bear

Chicken Mole Poblano

Serves the multitudes – leftover sauce freezes well.

8 roast chickens – I buy them at Costco
8 packages of flour tortillas
1 recipe mole sauce

For the mole sauce:
4 cups chicken broth
1 cups blanched almonds
2 Tbsp. crushed, dried hot chilies
$\frac{1}{2}$ cup sesame seeds
$1\frac{1}{2}$ tsp. ground cinnamon
$\frac{1}{4}$ tsp. ground cloves
$\frac{1}{2}$ tsp. each ground coriander seed, ground cumin, anise seeds
1 14-oz. can chopped tomatoes with juice
1 cup raisins
4 small fresh hot chilies
1 large onion, chopped
1 Tbsp. sugar
$\frac{1}{2}$ tsp. freshly ground black pepper
2-4 squares unsweetened chocolate

In a food processor, puree 2 cups broth, almonds, dried chilies, sesame seeds, cinnamon, cloves, coriander seed, cumin, and anise seeds. Pour in to heavy, large saucepan.

Puree tomatoes, raisins, fresh chilies, onion, sugar, and pepper, and add to mixture in saucepan. Add remaining broth and 2 squares of chocolate, and bring mixture to a simmer, stirring occasionally. Taste and add salt as needed. After the chocolate has melted, taste to see if it needs more chocolate – I usually go with the full 4 squares, as I like the deep note that it brings to the flavor. Simmer, stirring now and then, for about 30 minutes. Set aside until ready to serve.

Strip the meat from the chicken and tear into generous shreds, arranging artfully on two large-rimmed baking sheets. If you need to keep things warm until you are ready to serve, pour the juices over the meat, loosely cover with foil, and retain in a 200 degree oven.

Wrap the contents of one package of tortillas at a time in a clean dishcloth, and put in microwave for 1 or 2 minutes.

Arrange the serving dishes so that guests place a warm tortilla on their plate, take a portion of chicken, then drizzle the mole sauce over it generously. Roll it up and eat, and come back for more!

Serves a crowd

Janey Bennett

Research for *The Pale Surface of Things* led Janey Bennett into the study of classical Greek. Her interest spread to Byzantine icon painting, the sociology of Greek villages, Minoan culture and art, the science of archaeology, World War II on Crete, and criminal law in Greece. All this led directly to Cretan cooking. She has been writing fiction for eight years. Her writings on architecture have been published in the United States and Finland, where she held a Fulbright research fellowship.

ABOUT THE RECIPE:

"Mboureki is claimed as Chania, Crete's special dish. My novel, *The Pale Surface of Things,* takes place in Chania and the mountains above it. What better recipe to offer than the favorite one of the area?

It is true that Mboureki (Burek, Börek, Boereg, Brik) crops up in other places, (some say it shows up all across the former Ottoman Empire), but ask the citizens of Chania and they'll tell you it's their city's specialty. There are many variations, even within Chania, but most of them include potato, zucchini, mint, and cheese, with or without a crust."

– Janey Bennett

Mboureki from Chania, Crete

1 package of phyllo pastry, thawed
3 zucchini, sliced ½ inch thick
2 Russet (baking) potatoes, peeled, parboiled, and sliced ½ inch thick.
⅓ cup Cretan olive oil (greenish in color and wonderfully fragrant!!)
Salt, pepper, and oregano
4 - 6 oz. sheep's-milk feta cheese
Greek yoghurt
½ cup of fresh mint, chopped
1 Tbsp. melted butter

Preheat oven to 350 degrees.

Drape sheets of phyllo pastry across and over the edge of a shallow baking dish. (*Running late?* Skip the phyllo. It's still mboureki!)

Spread half the zucchini slices and half the parboiled potato slices across the bottom. Scatter half the crumbled feta cheese over them, dot with spoonfuls of Greek yoghurt, and scatter half the mint pieces over that.

Turn the rest of the sliced potatoes and zucchini in the olive oil and spices. Then, layer them on top of the mint. Put the remaining feta, yoghurt and mint on that layer, and then fold the overlapping phyllo pastry over the sides. The center of the cheese and yoghurt will still show through. Brush the phyllo with melted butter.

Bake at 350 degrees until potatoes are done, usually one hour or a bit more, depending on the potatoes. In traditional villages, the baker has the only oven, so baked dishes are cooked there (after he makes the day's bread), and served later at room temperature. Letting them sit gives the flavors a chance to blend.

Serves 6

Elizabeth Berg

On *The New York Times* Bestseller List multiple times, Elizabeth Berg writes books with wide appeal. *Durable Goods* and *Joy School* were both selected as American Library Association Best Book of the Year. *Open House* was an Oprah's Book Club Selection. Her books have been translated into 26 languages. Three television movies have been made from *Range of Motion*, *Open House* and *Say When*.

PUBLISHED WORKS:

The Day I Ate Whatever I Wanted: And Other Small Acts of Liberation, Dream When You're Feeling Blue, We Are All Welcome Here, The Handmaid and the Carpenter, The Year of Pleasures, The Art of Mending, Say When, True to Form, Never Change, Ordinary Life, Escaping into the Open: The Art of Writing True, Open House, Until the Real Thing Comes Along, What We Keep, Joy School, The Pull of the Moon, Range of Motion, Talk Before Sleep, Durable Goods and *Family Traditions.*

ABOUT THE RECIPE:

"I know these sound weird, but they're really good! I make these ALL THE TIME!"
— *Elizabeth Berg*

Chocolate Mint Brownies

$1/2$ cup flour
4 oz. package chocolate fudge instant pudding mix
$1/2$ tsp. baking powder
$1/4$ tsp. salt
$2/3$ cup sugar
3 Tbsp. butter
1 egg
1 egg white
¼ cup baby food prunes
1 tsp. peppermint extract
$1/3$ cup mini chocolate chips

Preheat the oven to 350 degrees. Mix flour, pudding mix, baking powder and salt and set aside. Mix sugar, butter, egg and egg white on medium speed of an electric mixer. Add prunes and peppermint extract and beat again. Add flour mixture and beat until smooth. Fold in chocolate chips. Spread evenly in prepared baking pan. Bake 30-35 minutes, until dry to touch and puffy. Let cool before cutting into squares.

Yield: 12 brownies

Chelsea Cain

Beginning the first few years of her life on an Iowa commune, Chelsea Cain then grew up in Bellingham, Washington, where the infamous Green River killer was "the boogeyman" of her youth. Her first novel featuring Detective Archie Sheridan and killer Gretchen Lowell, *Heartsick*, was a *New York Times* bestseller. The author of *Confessions of a Teenage Sleuth*, a parody based on the life of Nancy Drew, several nonfiction titles, and a weekly column in *The Oregonian*, Chelsea Cain now lives in Portland with her family. Visit her online at www.chelseacain.com.

ABOUT THE RECIPE:

"I now live in Portland, Oregon and never learned to cook. I did, however learn the telephone number of several outstanding local pizzerias. Enjoy."

– Chelsea Cain

Pizza a la Chelsea Cain

1 healthy cup laziness
The telephone number of your local fine pizza establishment
Approximately $25, with tip
Salt and pepper (to taste)

Telephone your local fine pizza establishment. Place an order for a large pizza with basil pesto, smoked mozzarella, roasted red potatoes, squash and red onions. Provide your name, address and telephone number, as well as method of payment. Wait 45 minutes for delivery. When the doorbell rings, answer door. Accept delivery. Sign for credit card, or pay cash. Don't forget to generously tip your delivery person.

Carry pizza to kitchen counter.

Carefully open pizza box.

Feel guilty about not having a side salad. Tell yourself the squash on the pizza would make a salad redundant.

Remove one slice of pizza and place it on a plate, preferably paper.

Leave pizza box open.

Get lectured by your husband about how important it is to close the pizza box to preserve heat.

Close the pizza box.

Season pizza slice with salt and pepper to taste.

On special occasions, serve with fork and knife.

Re-heat leftovers, 2 min per slice. Microwave times and temperatures may vary. Conventional ovens will preserve the integrity of the pizza, but may add up to ten long minutes to the reheat process.

Note: This meal goes best with TV, but is remarkably adaptable.

Deb Caletti

Award-winning author Deb Caletti has written *The Queen of Everything; Honey, Baby, Sweetheart; Wild Roses; The Nature of Jade* and *The Fortunes of Indigo Skye.* In addition to being a National Book Award finalist, Deb's work has gained other distinguished recognition, including the PNBA Best Book Award, the Washington State Book Award and School Library Journal's Best Book Award, and finalist citations for the California Young Reader Medal and the PEN USA Literary Award. Her sixth book, *The Secret Life of Prince Charming,* will be released in 2009. Paul G. Allen's Vulcan Productions and Infinity Features (makers of "Capote") have recently partnered to bring all five of Caletti's novels to film. Deb grew up in the San Francisco Bay Area and now lives with her family outside of Seattle.

PUBLISHED WORKS:

The Queen of Everything; Honey, Baby, Sweetheart; Wild Roses; The Nature of Jade; The Fortune of Indigo Skye and *The Secret Life of Prince Charming.*

ABOUT THE RECIPE:

"When you're in dire need for five gajillion instantly satisfying fat calories, these are the cookies for you. This recipe has been quelling cookie cravings in my family for many years – the original is written in my grandmother's handwriting on the back of a piece of junk mail, which is now frail and taped together and thoroughly splotched with ingredients, as a good recipe should be. Unless you want to be eating dough and making cookies all day (and we do have those days), then I'd suggest halving the recipe. I dare you to have only one. I dare you."

– Deb Caletti

Grandma-Mom's Sugar Cookies

Cream together:
1 cup powdered sugar
1 cup granulated sugar
1 cup butter

Add:
1 cup oil
2 eggs, beaten
2 tsp. vanilla
5 cups flour
1 tsp. soda
1 tsp. cream of tartar
¼ tsp. salt

Roll into small balls. Press with cookie press or glass bottom dipped in sugar. Sprinkle sugar on top.

Bake in a 350-degree oven for 10-12 minutes.

Serves 1 - 12

Stella Cameron

The New York Times best-selling, prize-winning author of more than 60 novels, Stella Cameron is prolific. She is the recipient of the Pacific Northwest Award for Literary Achievement. English by birth and a longtime Seattleite, Stella happily trips over the many authors who crawl out from every rock she turns over in the area and wouldn't live anywhere else. With her husband, Jerry, one dog (for now) and one cat (for now), she spends much of her spare time researching desperate issues such as how to save small dogs' teeth. Politically a centrist (and fearless), she invites inflammatory ideas from all sides. Visit Stella at www.stellacameron.com and www.runningwithquills.

PUBLISHED WORKS:

Kiss Them Goodbye, Now You See Him, A Grave Mistake, Body of Evidence, A Marked Man, Target, A Cold Day in Hell and *Cypress Nights.*

ABOUT THE RECIPE:

"A small English seaside town, a pale sun struggling valiantly, sand between my teeth and my toes and the coveted frosty dish before me on the ice cream parlor counter. Bliss. A cherished recollection from childhood days that became a special treat for our own children."

– Stella Cameron

Knickerbockerglory
(Or, Knickerblockergloria as our son called them when he was little.)

EQUIPMENT:
A large sundae glass for each person
A very, very long spoon – for each person
An ice cream scoop
Large number of napkins

INGREDIENTS:
Various flavors of ice cream
Various flavors of syrup
Nuts
Fruit: blueberries, pineapple chunks, chocolate chips from a chocolate chip bush, apricots, fresh mango, guava, lilikoi, bananas, strawberries, blackberries, Marino berries, lingenberries, red currants, black currants, gooseberries, loganberries. This list is a list of possibilities. You don't have to use all of them at the same time.

SUNDRIES:
M&Ms, Oreo crumbles, Butterfinger bits, raisins (sorry, that belongs with fruits really, I think), sprinkles, tubes of frosting in color of choice. Cherries, whipped cream

Gob of syrup in bottom of glass
Scoop of ice cream
Toss in nuts and fruit
Another gob of syrup – I suggest a different flavor
Scoop of ice cream – I suggest a different flavor
Toss in nuts and fruit
Another gob of syrup – time for the third flavor
Scoop of ice cream – I suggest a different flavor
Toss in nuts and fruit
Another gob of syrup – fourth flavor–let this drip down through ice cream, fruit and nuts a bit.
Final scoop of ice cream. Vanilla is recommended here to clean palate before the blast to come.
Nuts, Oreo crumbles, Butterfinger crumbles
Final gob of syrup – plenty, please.
Whipped cream to adequate point
Sprinkles
Cherry on top
Tube of frosting is to write name of recipient, if you can find somewhere to do this.

Serving suggestion: Three times a day

Kathy Casey

Celebrity chef Kathy Casey is widely recognized for her role in bringing women chefs and Northwest cuisine to national prominence. She is hailed for her ability to dazzle the palate and for her creative cocktail development work.

She owns Kathy Casey Food Studios, a food, beverage, and restaurant consulting company and special events venue in Seattle. With her husband John, she co-owns Dish D'Lish, her fresh-made "Food T' Go Go" concept and line of specialty products. The Dish D'Lish flagship café and store is in the Seattle neighborhood of Ballard plus two locations at SeaTac International Airport.

Kathy is a frequent TV guest and speaker on trends. She is a columnist and an established cookbook author; her newest is *Kathy Casey's Northwest Table*. A true Northwesterner, this Washington-born chef grows an urban "parking lot" garden and loves to fish and hunt wild mushrooms and berries. For recipes, Dish D'Lish products and the latest buzz, visit www.kathycasey.com.

PUBLISHED WORKS:

Kathy Casey's Northwest Table, Star Palate: Celebrity Cookbook for a Cure, Retro Food Fiascos: A collection of curious concoctions, Dishing with Kathy Casey: Food, Fun & Cocktails from Seattle's Culinary Diva, Best Places Seattle Cookbook (with Cynthia Nims), *Kathy Casey Cooks Favorites,* and *Pacific Northwest: The Beautiful Cookbook.*

ABOUT THE RECIPE:

"This is my favorite salad! The unique dressing has a beautiful ruby red color and a sweet and tangy flavor that's a perfect counterbalance to the spicy walnuts and refreshing Asian pears. I love to serve this bright and festive salad during the fall and winter holidays. And, the dressing is so good you will want to put it over everything, including slices of leftover cold turkey."

– Kathy Casey

Seasonal Greens with Spicy Walnuts, Crisp Asian Pears & Cranberry Vinaigrette

SPICY WALNUTS:
1 1/2 tsp. butter, melted
1/8 tsp. cayenne
1/8 tsp. ground cinnamon
2 Tbsp. honey
1/4 tsp. salt
1/2 cup coarsely chopped walnuts

SALAD:
8 cups mixed seasonal greens
1 large or 2 small Asian pears, quartered, cored and sliced into 1/8 inch
    wedges
1/2 small red onion, thinly sliced
Cranberry Vinaigrette (recipe follows)

TO MAKE THE SPICY WALNUTS: Combine all of the walnut ingredients in a small skillet and toss well to coat. Cook over medium heat until nuts are lightly browned. Remove from heat and let cool, stirring frequently to keep the nuts from sticking together.

TO ASSEMBLE THE SALAD: Toss the seasonal greens, Asian pear, and onions with some of the Cranberry Vinaigrette until well coated. Divide among individual salad plates. Top the salads with Spicy Walnuts and pass the extra vinaigrette.

CRANBERRY VINAIGRETTE
Makes 1^1/$_2$ cups

^{2}/$_3$ cup fresh or frozen cranberries
^{1}/$_4$ cup sugar
^{1}/$_2$ cup white wine or distilled vinegar
1 tsp. Dijon mustard
^{1}/$_4$ cup orange juice
^{3}/$_4$ cup vegetable oil or very light olive oil
^{1}/$_4$ tsp. salt
^{1}/$_4$ tsp. black pepper

Place the cranberries, sugar, and vinegar in a small saucepan. Cook over medium heat until the cranberries pop, in about 4 to 5 minutes. Remove from heat and let cool. Purée the cranberry mixture in a blender.

Pour the purée into a medium bowl and whisk in the mustard and orange juice. Gradually whisk in the oil, a little at a time. The dressing should become smooth and emulsified. Season with salt and pepper. Refrigerate until needed.

Makes 4 to 6 salad servings

Recipe from *Dishing with Kathy Casey: Food, Fun & Cocktails from Seattle's Culinary Diva*, Sasquatch Books, Seattle. Copyright © 2002 by Kathy Casey.

Dale Chihuly

Born in 1941 in Tacoma, Washington, Dale Chihuly was introduced to glass while studying interior design at the University of Washington. In 1968, Chihuly was awarded a Fulbright Fellowship to work at the Venini factory in Venice, Italy. In 1971, he co-founded Pilchuck Glass School, in Stanwood, Washington. With this international glass center, Chihuly led the avant-garde in the development of glass blowing as a studio art and the broader contemporary interest in glass as an expressive medium. His work can be seen in collections at more than 200 museums worldwide. His most-recent published titles include *Chihuly Black*, *Team Chihuly*, and *Fire · Dale Chihuly*.

ABOUT THE RECIPE:

"This recipe is a combination of ingredients from all of the great Italian glass blowers that I know."

– Dale Chihuly

Dale's Pasta Sauce

2 large cans (28 oz. each) Roma tomatoes
2 medium sprigs fresh rosemary
½ lb. fresh Shiitake mushrooms (sliced)
1 medium red onion (minced)
1 Tbsp. garlic (chopped)
2 fresh celery stalks (chopped)
2 Tbsp. fresh thyme (chopped)
2 Tbsp. fresh oregano (chopped)
2 cans (14.5 oz. each) vegetable stock
1 cup white wine
½ cup extra virgin olive oil
½ cube butter
1 tsp. crushed red pepper
1 jar (10 oz.) roasted red peppers (drained and chopped)

In a deep saucepan, bring olive oil to a medium-high temperature and add minced onion, chopped garlic, and rosemary. Sauté until limp. Add celery and mushrooms and continue to sauté a few moments longer. Add tomatoes (be sure to crush them throughout the cooking process), oregano, thyme, vegetable stock, wine, crushed red pepper, and roasted red pepper.

Bring pot to a boil. Reduce heat. Cook until sauce is reduced by a third (or, is heavy and thick). Approximate cooking time is 2 hours.

When sauce is finished, add the butter and stir until well incorporated. Adjust seasonings to taste. Add the pasta of your choice and enjoy.

Serves 6 – 8

Curt Colbert

The author of the Jake Rossiter and Miss Jenkins mysteries, Curt Colbert has created a series of hardboiled, private detective novels set in 1940s Seattle. The first book, *Rat City*, was nominated for a Shamus Award. A Seattle native, Curt is also a poet and an avid history buff. He is currently finishing the fourth book in the series, *Nowhere Town,* and recently served as the editor of the upcoming short-story anthology, *Seattle Noir,* that will be released in 2009.

ABOUT THE RECIPE:

"This recipe for bruschetta [brus ket:a] was created because of my love for Italian food. In fact, when I found out about real Italian cooking, it was much the same as when I first learned to read – I just couldn't get enough. The endless adventures of books and Italian cuisine were addictive.

Of course, I found out about books long before my exposure to true Italian food. Like many Americans, I thought Italian dining was limited to spaghetti and meatballs, lasagna, pizza, red and white checkered tablecloths, and Chianti bottles covered with candle-drippings. Early on, however, my own cooking skills were limited to boiling water, which worked very well indeed for packaged Kraft® macaroni & cheese.

Luckily, I learned more about cooking as the years went on. I was fortunate enough to get a first taste of classic bruschetta in San Francisco while traveling for a Seattle-based food distributor. It was a revelation – simply toasted bread, a little basil and garlic, olive oil with fresh plum tomatoes. Who knew it could be so good? The food broker with whom I was dining conducted the rest of the meal like a guided tour of some of the various regions in Italy. I was hooked.*

Fortunately, I had overcome any fear of cooking due to a stint as the head cook in a seafood restaurant before I started selling food for a living. I found that you had to approach cooking with confidence – most anything you start timidly has a good chance of turning out tepidly. The worst that can happen if you blow a recipe is that you have to eat it. But if you succeed with a recipe, the best that can happen is that you and others will enjoy eating it. So I always approach new recipes with gusto and confidence."

– Curt Colbert

Hearty Bruschetta

1 small can Italian-recipe stewed tomatoes (more robust than fresh
    tomatoes)
3-4 cloves garlic, coarsely chopped (not minced)
3-4 Tbsp. extra-virgin olive oil
1 cup shredded, low-moisture mozzarella cheese
1/4 cup grated Parmesan (Reggiano or domestic) cheese
Capers (nonpareil)
1 baguette, sliced thin (1/4 inch thick or slightly less)

1. Thoroughly drain the can of Italian stewed tomatoes. Coarsely chop tomatoes into approximately 1/4 inch chunks.
2. Lightly toast baguette slices on both sides under a fairly close broiler.
3. Combine chopped garlic with olive oil and sauté until garlic turns medium brown. Quickly remove from heat as garlic may otherwise burn.
4. Arrange toasted baguette slices on broiler pan or baking sheet. Brush top of each with the oil mixture (make sure every slice also gets a few pieces of browned garlic).
5. Put 3 or 4 capers on each baguette slice.
6. Distribute tomato pieces on the baguette slices (5 or 6 pieces for each).
7. Sprinkle shredded mozzarella on each slice (just enough to cover; not too heavy).
8. Dust with a little grated Parmesan.
9. Toast the finished bruschetta under a fairly close broiler until cheese has melted and is slightly browned. Alternatively, finish in a 425 to 450 degree oven – top rack – for 4 to 5 minutes.

Makes about 20 to 24 small slices – will serve 6-10 as an appetizer.

* One of the premier food importers in the region, "Big John" Croce, gave me a continuing appreciation for Italian cuisine.

Ann Kondo Corum

Hawai'ian cookbook author and illustrator Ann Corum applies her culinary expertise to present lively and humorous specialty cookbooks dedicated to the Island standby, SPAM®. Corum was born in Honolulu and graduated from Punahou School. She has a degree in English from California State University at Long Beach and a MS degree from the University of Southern California. She is also the author-illustrator of *Easy Cooking the Island Way, Only in Hawai'i, Hawai'i's SPAM Cookbook*, and *Hawai'i's 2nd SPAM Cookbook*, as well as two books for children, *Aunty Pua's Keiki Cookbook* and *Aunty Pua's Dilemma*.

Corum's humorous cartoons about island life enhance her delightful, bestselling books celebrating healthful, local-style meals using this versatile, all-purpose canned meat. This traditional staple is showcased Hawai'ian-style in hundreds recipes ranging from Fried Rice SPAM Musubi, Pita Pocket SPAM, and Chinese-Style SPAM Paella, to SPAM Quiche, Seared SPAM with Hawai'ian Slaw, and Korean-Style SPAM. With Corum's second Hawai'i's *SPAM Cookbook II* release, she offers another culinary wealth of ideas and entrées. Her collection presents illustrated recipes incorporating local foods and flavors. She showcases recipes for *pupus*, main dishes, rice and noodle dishes, breakfast and brunch favorites, quick and easy meals, and miscellaneous munchies – all made with SPAM.

ABOUT THE RECIPE:

"My illustrated recipe featuring SPAM, America's favorite canned meat, is more than a lunchtime staple. In the Hawai'ian Islands, it is revered and has become a way of life for many locals. In addition to this recipe, I suggest you explore the delights of SPAM and make Hawai'i-style appetizers, main dishes, rice and noodle dishes, breakfast and brunch favorites, quick and easy meals and miscellaneous munchies.

After all, with more than 60 million SPAM-ers in this country alone and countless others around the world, who knows where this will all end? It is safe to say that if you send this very Hawai'ian of gifts to friends far and wide – SPAM-mania will spread even further. By the way, did you know that more than four million cans are sold in Hawai'i alone each year – six cans per person – the highest rate in the country!"

– *Ann Kondo Corum*

Fried Rice SPAM Musubi

2 cups cooked Asian sticky rice
Ume slices (Japanese apricot, is a species of Asian plum)
1 can SPAM
Nori (dried sea plant for wrapping)

Notes: Haoles, you must use Calrose rice, not minute rice so it will stick together. A helpful hint for making SPAM-shaped musubi from the wisdom of Billy Apele: "Save your SPAM can, pat the rice in the can and then dump it out. Be careful. The edges of the can are sharp!"

Make individual musubi rice cakes as usual, except make them oblong (SPAM-shape). Remove Spam from can, slice and fry it until it is browned. Cut nori into strips 2-3 inches wide and long enough to go around the musubi. Place a piece of SPAM on top of the rice and wrap nori around it. Garnish with ume.

Serves 4

Mary Daheim

Seattle native Mary Richardson Daheim has been fascinated by story telling since early childhood. She first listened, then read, and finally began to write her own fiction when she was ten. A journalism major at the University of Washington, she was the first female editor of *The Daily* where she attracted national attention with her editorial stance against bigotry.

After gaining her degree, she worked in newspapers and public relations, and in her spare time she tried her hand at novels. In 1983, Daheim's first historical romance was published, followed by a half-dozen more before she switched genres to her original fictional love, mysteries. *Just Desserts* and *Fowl Prey*, the first two of 24 books in the Bed-and-Breakfast series, were released in 1991, and the most recent, *Vi Agra Falls*, was published in 2008. In 1992, the Emma Lord series made its debut with *The Alpine Advocate*. The nineteenth, *The Alpine Traitor*, was published in 2008. Daheim has also written several short stories for mystery anthologies and magazines.

Married to professor emeritus David Daheim, the couple lives in Seattle and has three grown daughters. She has been an Agatha Award nominee, winner of the 2000 Pacific Northwest Writers Association Achievement Award, and her mysteries regularly make the *USA Today* bestseller list and *The New York Times* top thirty.

ABOUT THE RECIPE:

"I've never poisoned anybody yet (though I could, owning a couple of books on how to do it – strictly for research, of course, but I'd probably screw it up, taste the stuff, and off myself instead). This recipe is for the Clemans family's utterly wonderful potato rolls – they owned the mill in Alpine and the town itself. These rolls were served in the real Alpine way back when, now served at all our family holiday gatherings. Yum!"

– Mary Daheim

Alpine Potato Rolls

1 cup mashed potatoes
$^1/_2$ cup shortening
$^1/_2$ cup sugar
1 tsp. salt
1 cup warmed milk
1 yeast cake or packet dissolved in $^1/_3$ cup lukewarm water
1 cup flour
2 eggs
1 more cup flour

Knead with vigor or use dough mixer attachment. Let rise 2 hours at room temperature covered with a damp cloth. Add $3^1/_2$ cups more flour. Knead again as directed above. Refrigerate overnight. Roll out and use round cutter; fold each roll over once. Put on baking sheets.

Bake at 450 degrees for approximately 10 minutes, but watch closely as bottoms of rolls can get too well done.

Debra Dean

Born and raised in Seattle, Debra Dean is the daughter of a builder and a home-maker and artist. She was a bookworm at an early age but never imagined becoming a writer.

Debra Dean's first novel, *The Madonnas of Leningrad*, was published in March 2006 and is being released in more than a dozen languages. It was a *New York Times* Editors' Choice, a Borders Original Voice, and a #1 Booksense Pick, as well as a finalist for the Quill Award and the Guardian First Book Award (UK). Her short fiction has appeared in *Mid-American Review, Image, The Seattle Review, Calyx, Writers Forum*, and *The Bellingham Review* and has won awards including the Association of Writers and Writing Programs Intro Journals Award and the Nelson Bentley Prize.

Debra Dean worked as an actor in the New York theater for nearly a decade before opting for the more secure life of a writer. She and her husband now live in Miami, where she is teaching at the University of Miami. She is currently at work on her second novel.

PUBLISHED WORKS:

Confessions of a Falling Woman and *The Madonnas of Leningrad.*

ABOUT THE RECIPE:

"These biscotti are lovely, dense and a bit chewy. I was given the recipe by a fellow writer when we were in grad school together. Over the years, I've improvised any number of variations, replacing the anise with the zest of an orange or dried cherries and almond extract, etc. I used to have a recurring fantasy of making my way in the world by supplying these biscotti to coffee shops, but I've restricted my little cottage industry to a few weeks at the holidays baking them for friends and family around the country."

– Debra Dean

Biscotti

3³/₄ cups flour
2¹/₂ cups sugar
1 tsp. baking powder
Pinch salt
4 eggs at room temperature, lightly beaten (or use egg substitute)
2 egg yolks, room temperature.
2 tsp. crushed anise seed
1 tsp. vanilla
1²/₃ cups raw almonds, toasted and roughly cut

Mix flour, sugar, salt, baking powder, and anise. In separate bowl, mix 3 of the eggs, egg yolks, vanilla, and orange zest if desired.

Make a deep well in the center of the flour mixture. Into this, pour the wet ingredients. Gradually work ingredients into flour. Mix with hands (messy, but necessary: take off your rings first!). Knead in almonds. Dough is very sticky – don't add more flour or water.

Use parchment or butter and flour a baking sheet. Divide dough in half and shape into 2¹/₂" wide flattened logs (lightly flour your hands). Place at least 2" apart on floured surface. Beat remaining egg and lightly brush over logs.

Bake 35 minutes at 350 degrees. Allow to cool (10-15 minutes). Cut diagonally into ³/₄-1" slices. (If slices are too thick, the second bake will leave them soft, if too thin, too crunchy). Bake slices, face up at 325 degrees for 7-10 minutes on each side.

Jo Dereske

Originally from a Lithuanian family in Mason County, a rural area of western Michigan, Jo Dereske has lived in the Bellingham, Washington-area for more than thirty years.

"I was a closet writer from the time I could read but didn't believe I stood a chance since I wasn't from New York. I've been a librarian, a forest fire tower lookout, a waitress, a sheetrock finisher, a business owner, and best of all, a writer. I now live in the foothills of Mount Baker and have a totally independent and cranky dog I adore," said Dereske.

Best known for the Miss Zukas mysteries set in the fictional town of Bellehaven, Washington, she has also written the Ruby Crane series of mysteries as well as three books for young people, including the fantasy *Glom Gloom*.

"I've drawn heavily on my Lithuanian background and my love for the oddities of the library world for the Miss Zukas series. Forgery, always a an interest since I forged by first absence excuse in fourth grade, figures heavily in the Ruby Crane series," added Dereske.

PUBLISHED WORKS:

Glom Gloom, The Lone Sentinel and *My Cousin the Poodle*. There are eleven books in the Miss Zukas mystery series and three books in the Ruby Crane mystery series.

ABOUT THE RECIPE:

"I've had this recipe since I was a child. I think it's from an aunt, but it's always a crowd-pleaser. It forms its own lemon sauce and has a light, elegant taste. The trick is to be sure to bake it in a pan of water."

— Jo Dereske

Lemon Pudding Cake

2 eggs, separated
1 tsp. grated lemon peel
¼ cup lemon juice
⅔ cup milk
1 cup sugar
½ cup flour
¼ tsp. salt

Beat egg whites until stiff. Set aside. Beat egg yolks. Blend in lemon peel, lemon juice and milk. Add sugar, flour and salt. Beat until smooth, then fold into egg whites. Pour into ungreased 1-quart casserole dish. Place casserole in pan of very hot water.

Bake 50 minutes, or until golden brown, at 350 degrees.

Serves 3-4

William Dietrich

Pulitzer Prize-winning journalist, historian and naturalist, William Dietrich was born in 1951 and grew up in Tacoma, Washington. A journalism graduate from Fairhaven College at Western Washington University, where he now is a part-time professor, Dietrich has spent most of his life in the Pacific Northwest, with briefer sojourns in Washington, D.C. and Boston. He spent a year at Harvard University at the Nieman fellowship program for journalists, was a fellow at the Woods Hole Marine Biological Laboratory in Massachusetts, and is also a staff writer for the *Pacific Northwest* magazine at *The Seattle Times*. Dietrich is married, has two college-age daughters, and lives in Anacortes, Washington.

PUBLISHED WORKS:

The Dakota Cipher (March, 2009), The Rosetta Key, Napoleon's Pyramids, On Puget Sound, The Scourge of God, Hadrian's Wall, Natural Grace, Dark Winter, Getting Back, Ice Reich, Northwest Passage and *The Final Forest.*

ABOUT THE RECIPE:

"We originally had this dessert more than a quarter-century ago at Portland's Genoa restaurant. It is so sublime, so decadent, so seductive, and so downright erotic that consuming it probably means eternal damnation. But it's worth it. Not simple to make, but great for special occasions, and surprisingly light – until you have seconds. By the way, I don't make this – I have difficulty with toaster waffles – but my wife occasionally spoils me with 'Boccone Dolce,' or 'Sweet Mouthful.'"

– *Bill Dietrich*

Boccone Dolce

6 egg whites, room temperature
Pinch of salt
¼ tsp. cream of tartar
1½ cups sugar
5 oz. semisweet chocolate
2-3 Tbsp. water
3 cups whipping cream, whipped very stiffly
1½ pints of berries, such as sliced strawberries, raspberries, blueberries or a combination of these
6-8 whole berries as garnish on the top

Preheat oven to 250 degrees.

Beat egg whites with salt until foamy. Add cream of tartar and beat until soft peaks form. Gradually beat in sugar until meringue is stiff and glossy.

Line baking sheets with greased wax paper and trace three circles, 8 inches in diameter. Evenly spread or pipe the meringue onto the circles. Bake 1 hour. Turn off the heat and let the meringues dry in the oven for another hour. Remove from oven and carefully peel off waxed paper. Let cool completely on wire racks.

Melt chocolate with water in top of double boiler and stir until smooth. Spread over two of the meringue layers and let stand until set.

To assemble: Place one meringue circle, chocolate side up, on a serving plate. Spread with ½-inch layer of whipped cream. Cover with about half the berries. Repeat with second chocolate-covered layer. Top with plain meringue and frost entire cake with remaining whipped cream.

Garnish with whole berries and refrigerate for 6-to-24 hours. Cut carefully – but even if it crumbles, it's delicious.

Serves 6 - 8

Tom Douglas

Along with his wife and business partner, Jackie Cross, Tom Douglas owns five of Seattle's most exciting restaurants: Dahlia Lounge (nominated for Best Restaurant by the James Beard Association in 2006), Etta's, Palace Kitchen (nominated for Best New Restaurant by the James Beard Association in 1997), Lola, and Serious Pie. In addition, Tom runs a retail bakery, a catering business and the Palace Ballroom.

Over the course of more than 20 years, the media has highlighted Tom as the Seattle chef who has been instrumental in defining the Northwest Style. Tom's creativity with local ingredients and his respect for Seattle's ethnic traditions have helped him win numerous awards and accolades including the James Beard Award for Best Northwest Chef in 1994.

He is the author of three cookbooks, *Tom Douglas' Seattle Kitchen,* which won a James Beard award for Best Americana Cookbook, *Tom's Big Dinners* and *I Love Crab Cakes.* In addition, Tom's specialty food line of spice rubs plus barbecue and teriyaki sauces is sold nationwide. Tom also hosts his own weekly talk radio show, Tom Douglas' Seattle Kitchen, on local KIRO radio.

ABOUT THE RECIPE:

"A favorite lunch when I was growing up was my mom's creamy tomato soup. She liked to cut buttered toast into squares and float them atop each soup bowl, and that was the best part. Nowadays, we serve my version of the soup at the Dahlia Lounge and Dahlia Bakery with brown butter croutons that are nice and buttery and not too crisp, still a bit soft inside – like mom's buttered toast squares."

– Tom Douglas

Tom's Favorite Tomato Soup with Brown Butter Croutons

1 Tbsp. butter
1 Tbsp. olive oil
1 medium onion, thinly sliced
3 cloves garlic, smashed with the side of your knife
5 cups canned whole tomatoes in juice
1 cup water
$2/3$ cup heavy cream
2 tsp. kosher salt
$1/4$ tsp. black pepper
$1/4$ tsp. crushed red pepper flakes
$1/4$ tsp. celery seed
$1/4$ tsp. dried oregano
1 Tbsp. sugar

For the brown butter croutons:
2 tsp. butter
2 tsp. olive oil
4 slices bread (such as European style rustic bread), crusts trimmed,
    cut into $3/4$ inch cubes

Heat the butter and olive oil in a large saucepan and sauté the onion and garlic five minutes, or until translucent. Add the tomatoes, water, cream, herbs, spices and sugar. Bring to a boil, then turn down to a simmer and simmer for 15 minutes. Remove from the heat and puree in batches in a blender. Return the soup to the pot and reheat to a simmer, seasoning to taste with salt and pepper.

Meanwhile, make the brown butter croutons. Heat the butter in a small pan over medium high heat until the butter begins to brown, a minute or two. Remove from the heat and set aside. In a sauté pan, heat the oil over medium high heat. Add the bread cubes and toast, stirring occasionally, until golden, about 6 to 8 minutes. Remove from the heat and stir in the browned butter.

Serve the soup garnished with the croutons. *Serves 6*

Robert Dugoni

A long-time practicing civil litigator in San Francisco and Seattle, Robert Dugoni is *The New York Times* and *San Francisco Chronicle* best-selling author of the legal thrillers. He has written *The Jury Master* and *Damage Control*, as well as the exposé, *The Cyanide Canary* – a *Washington Post* 2004 Best Book of the Year Selection and the Idaho Book of the Year. Robert is a two-time winner of the Pacific Northwest Writers Association Literary Award for fiction. He graduated *Phi Beta Kappa* from Stanford University with a degree in journalism and clerked as a reporter for *The Los Angeles Times* before obtaining is doctorate of jurisprudence from the University of California at Los Angeles School of Law.

ABOUT THE RECIPE:

"Every Christmas Eve for the past 45 years, my mother has cooked a special dinner of Italian gnocchi and for dessert her famous Christmas cream puffs. It's no small feat when cooking for 10 children, their spouses, and 27 grandchildren. The cream puffs are the highlight of the evening. If you've ever seen a feeding frenzy, you can picture her dinner table when the cream puffs are produced. I hope you enjoy them as much as we have for so many years."

– Robert Dugoni

Patty's Christmas Cream Puffs

Boil 1 cup water.
Add 1 cube butter and a pinch of salt.
After butter melts, add 1 cup of flour.
Remove from fire and use fork to stir it until it becomes a ball.
Beat in 4 eggs, one-at-a-time.

Put spoonful-size balls on a non-greased cookie sheet. Cook at 375 degrees for 20-25 minutes until brown. Don't remove too early or they'll collapse. Allow to cool.

Beat whipping cream with sugar and vanilla. Cut cream puffs in half, and pull out any excess dough. Fill with whipped cream.

Smear chocolate frosting on top and sprinkle with green and red topping for decoration.

Stuff in mouth one at a time until you feel sick! Go to bed and wait for Santa Claus.

Serves many!

Michelle Dunn

An internationally known expert and author on the topic of credit and collections, Michelle Dunn is a leading authority on collecting money for businesses. She is the author of several titles, including *Starting a Collection Agency, Become the Squeaky Wheel*, and *How to Get Your Customers to Pay*. Overseeing renowned authorities from the legal, financial, and accounting communities, she brings them all together to bring solutions and unique opportunities to every member of her Credit and Collections Association.

ABOUT THE RECIPE:

"I created this recipe last year when I started growing all of my own food. Being an entrepreneur, I like being independent, working from home and being self-sufficient. Creating healthy recipes from food I grow for my family is something that is very important to me. I am happy to share my fresh recipe with anyone who desires a healthier diet and lifestyle."

– Michelle Dunn

Radish Salsa

1 large mango or apple
2 or 3 apricots or dried cranberry, kiwi, blueberry, or strawberry
12 large radishes
Juice of 1 lime or lemon
2-3 Tbsp. virgin olive oil
Salt to taste
2-3 Tbsp. cilantro or mint

Chop all fruit, removing skins. Place in a large glass bowl.

Add radishes, citrus juice, olive oil, salt, and cilantro. If using mint, add immediately before serving to prevent mint from darkening. Mix well.

Cover and refrigerate for 2 hours or longer. Serve with grilled pork, fish, or chicken.

Valerie Easton

The author of four gardening books, Valerie Easton is a weekly garden columnist for *The Seattle Times' Pacific Northwest Magazine*. She contributes articles on gardens, homes and the people who make them to numerous publications including *Fine Gardening, Garden Design, Gardens Illustrated* and *Horticulture*. Valerie was a horticultural librarian for 18 years at the University of Washington, and is currently working on a garden murder mystery. She lives with her husband and a Wheaten Terrier in Seattle and on Whidbey Island where she's recently made a new garden, which was featured in *Horticulture* magazine and in *The New York Times*.

PUBLISHED WORKS:

Artists In Their Gardens; Plant Life: Growing a Garden in the Pacific Northwest and *A Pattern Garden: The Essential Elements of Garden-Making. The Simplified Garden*, Easton's new book, will be available in 2009.

ABOUT THE RECIPE:

"I have fond memories of this Greek lentil soup recipe, for a fellow librarian gave it to me during a slow night at the reference desk. It's packed with protein, is easily doubled, made in one pot, and tastes even better reheated the second night, so is an ideal dinner for a working mother of a vegetarian family. We all agree it's the best lentil soup, ever."

– Valerie Easton

Georgia's Greek Lentil Soup

Cover one cup of lentils with water. Boil three minutes and then drain.

Add:
6 cups water or vegetable stock
1 large stalk celery, sliced finely
1 large carrot, finely chopped
3 cloves garlic, minced
1 medium onion, finely chopped
$1/4$ cup good quality olive oil
1 tsp. salt
$1/2$ tsp. pepper
$3/4$ cup tomato sauce
1 bay leaf

Bring to a boil, cover and simmer 1-1$1/2$ hours. Remove the bay leaf. Add a little more water if needed.

Now here's the secret to why this soup is so good: Add 2-3 Tbsp. red wine vinegar and cook 10 minutes longer. Serve with a loaf of rosemary bread and a leafy green salad.

Aaron Elkins

Former anthropologist Aaron Elkins has been writing mysteries and thrillers since 1982, having won an Edgar for *Old Bones*, as well as a subsequent Agatha (with his wife Charlotte), and a Nero Wolfe Award. His major continuing series features forensic anthropologist-detective Gideon Oliver, "the skeleton detective."

His work is published in more than a dozen languages. He and his wife live on Washington's Olympic Peninsula, their marriage having survived (more or less intact) their collaboration on novels and short stories.

PUBLISHED WORKS:

Gideon Oliver Novels: *Uneasy Relations, Little Tiny Teeth, Unnatural Selection, Where There's A Will, Good Blood, Skeleton Dance, Twenty Blue Devils, Dead Men's Hearts, Make No Bones, Icy Clutches, Curses!, Old Bones, Murder in the Queen's Armes, The Dark Place, Fellowship of Fear.*

Chris Norgen Novels: *Old Scores, A Glancing Light, A Deceptive Clarity.*

Lee Ofsted Novels (with Charlotte Elkins) *On the Fringe, Where Have all the Birdies Gone?, Nasty Breaks, Rotten Lies, A Wicked Slice.*

Thrillers: *Turncoat* and *Loot.*

ABOUT THE RECIPE:

"I love a good table, and therefore, by God, my characters better be ready to eat. Most of my books have a couple of detailed dinner scenes, and quite a bit of the conversation seems to take place over meals and snacks. Here's one such snack, delicious and unusual. It's described in this passage from *Fellowship of Fear*. The scene is Heidelberg, Germany:

> *'For dinner he went to a sedate weinstübe that had been in business, according to its plaque outside, since 1677; its dark, polished wooden tables might have been its original furnishings. He made a richly satisfying meal from a bottle of Mosel wine and a plate of weißkäse, a buttery cheese served with little dishes of paprika and raw onions to mix into it.'*

"Well, it's practically as simple as it sounds, and here's a fine version."

– Aaron Elkins

Weißkäse

8 ounces cream cheese
2 tablespoons butter
2 tablespoons finely chopped onions
2 tablespoons caraway seed
1 tablespoon paprika

Whip together cream cheese and butter, shape into a mound, and put on serving plate. Set out with small dishes of onions, caraway seed, and paprika, and fold everything into the cheese just before the eating starts. (You could mix everything together in the kitchen first, but it's prettier this way.

Serve it with dark rye bread and beer or white wine.

A further note: "If you're watching your diet, Neufchatel or low-fat cream cheese and a low-fat butter substitute can do an okay (but not great) job of substituting for the cream cheese and butter. That's what I do. My characters, lucky devils, eat whatever they want."

– AE

Amply serves four as an appetizer.

Clyde W. Ford

Author, Clyde W. Ford is an award-winning creator of nonfiction and fiction titles. He is the recipient of the 2006 Hurston-Wright Legacy Award in Contemporary Fiction, a winner of the Independent Publishers Award for Best Thriller, and he received the 2006 Mahogany Media Award for Best Mystery. *Precious Cargo*, a nautical thriller and the second book of his Northwest suspense series, was re-released in hardback in 2008. He resides in Washington state.

PUBLISHED WORKS:

Nautical thrillers: *Red Herring, Precious Cargo* and *Whiskey Gulf* (available in 2009).
Shango mysteries: *The Long Mile* and *Deuce's Wild.*
Other works: *The Hero with an African Face, Compassionate Touch, Where Healing Waters Meet, We Can All Get Along* and *Boat Green.*

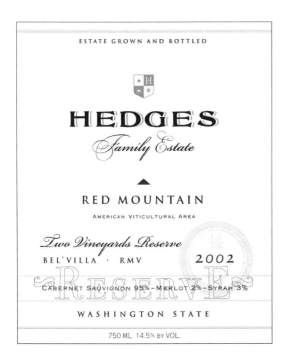

A BOOK AND A BOTTLE

"When I needed a wine for my Northwest suspense novels, *Red Herring* and *Precious Cargo*, I asked a local wine broker to name an expensive and elegant Washington State wine. He thought briefly, before saying, 'Hedges Red Mountain Reserve.' So I placed that wine in both books and made it a centerpiece of the romantic subplot.

Not long after *Red Herring* was first published, the wine broker heard that wine merchants in other parts of the state were being asked about Red Mountain Reserve. The vintner was trying to determine where this demand was coming from.

At first I couldn't imagine the publication of my book was responsible for a run on wine, until I gave a reading at a local book club in Tacoma and the organizer of the event lamented that he was only able to secure one bottle of Red Mountain Reserve. His wine merchant tried, but could not find any more in the state.

So, the wine broker and I hatched a scheme. I went to the restaurateur who owned the fine dining establishment where I'd set the ending scene of *Red Herring*. We contacted the Hedges Winery that agreed to ship us *gratis* two cases of Red Mountain Reserve from their private stock. And, we organized a reservation-only dinner/wine-tasting/book reading. The sittings were sold out within days of making the announcement.

After a wonderful meal, each person received a splash of Red Mountain Reserve. Then, as I read the passages from the book where my characters drank the wine, we all hoisted our glasses and drank along with them. And, what I realized as a novelist is that fiction and food are powerful ingredients to create community.

Rory Freedman & Kim Barnouin

A former modeling agent and a self-taught know-it-all, Rory Freedman, met up with Kim Barnouin, a former model who holds a MS degree in Holistic Nutrition. They quickly became fast friends. One of the foundations for their friendship was food – both were completely obsessed with it. So eventually, when they did change their ways, they experienced firsthand the difference a healthy diet could make. And the more they learned for themselves, the more they wanted to share their combined knowledge and help others. The result: *The New York Times* bestseller *Skinny Bitch: A no-nonsense, tough-love guide for savvy girls who want to stop eating crap and start looking fabulous!* Their second book, *Skinny Bitch in the Kitch: Kick-Ass Recipes for Hungry Girls Who Want to Stop Cooking Crap (and Start Looking Hot!)*, was published and is also a *New York Times* bestseller. A third book on healthy living during pregnancy – *Skinny Bitch: Bun in the Oven* – is now available, with *Skinny Bitchin'*, the program guide, available later. Not to overlook men, a book adapting the *Skinny Bitch* message for guys is on the horizon. For more information, visit www.skinnybitch.net.

ABOUT THE RECIPE:

"There is a common misconception that Skinny Bitch is all about deprivation. Nothing could be further from the truth. Skinny Bitch is the lifestyle we live.

And rest assured, we would never maintain it if we felt deprived. Whether it's shopping for food, talking about food, thinking about food, dreaming about food, cooking food, or eating food, we can't get enough. We devised the Skinny Bitch plan so we could have our cake and eat it! Try this new mac and cheese recipe and start looking great. If you don't experience multiple orgasms within the first three bites, you need to see your gyno."

– Rory Freedman

Macaroni and Four Cheeses

1 Tbsp. refined coconut oil, melted, or safflower oil, plus more
    for the casserole dish
About 2 Tbsp. fine sea salt
1 pound whole wheat or brown rice elbow macaroni
2 (10-oz.) packages frozen pureed winter squash
2 cups soy or rice milk
4 oz. vegan cheddar cheese, shredded
2 oz. vegan Jack cheese, shredded
4 oz. (about $\frac{1}{2}$ cup) vegan cream cheese
$1\frac{1}{2}$ tsp. powdered mustard
$\frac{1}{8}$ tsp. cayenne pepper
$\frac{1}{4}$ cup whole wheat bread crumbs
2 Tbsp. vegan Parmesan cheese

Preheat oven to 375 degrees. Oil a 2-quart casserole dish; set aside.

In a 4- to 6-quart stockpot over high heat, combine 3 quarts of water with about $1\frac{1}{2}$ tablespoons of the salt. Bring the water to a boil, add the macaroni, and cook according to the package directions.

Meanwhile, in a 3- to 4-quart saucepan over medium heat, combine the squash and milk, stirring and breaking up the squash with a spoon until the squash is defrosted. Increase the heat to medium-high and bring to a simmer, stirring occasionally. Remove from the heat and whisk in the cheddar, Jack, cream cheese, mustard, cayenne, and the remaining $\frac{1}{2}$ tablespoon of salt.

When the pasta is done, drain it, then return the pasta to the pot. Stir the cheese sauce into the macaroni. Transfer the entire mixture to the prepared baking pan.

In a medium bowl, combine the bread crumbs, Parmesan, and the 1 tablespoon of oil. Sprinkle over the top of the macaroni and cheese. Place the casserole dish on a baking sheet and bake for 20 minutes, then broil for 2 to 3 minutes, or until the top is nicely browned.

Serves 8

Felice Gerwitz

Involved in the world of publishing since the inception of her first book in 1992, Felice Gerwitz is an internationally recognized author. Her articles on the subjects of education have appeared in numerous magazines. Nine of her books were chosen for inclusion in "100 Top Picks for Homeschool Curriculum." *An Insider's Guide to Successful Science Fair Projects* was selected by God's World Publishing as the Book of the Month. Felice's ventures include starting a publishing company, an online field trips website, and an online seminar website, www.ScholarSquare.com. Felice is a popular conference speaker on a variety of educational topics and serves as a consultant to other authors.

ABOUT THE RECIPE

"My parents owned a bakery in New York, and later an Italian restaurant in Florida. I am a first generation Italian American, and have loved cooking from the time I was old enough to see the top of the stove. While I love to cook, baking is my passion and something I do to relax. When I begin baking, it often tends to be an all-day affair. Because I live a busy lifestyle, I often bake and freeze meals ahead of time. I have experimented through the years and have found several recipes that work well in this regard. One of my favorite make-ahead recipes is an apple cake.

This moist cake does well in the freezer for about 6 months. Of course it tastes best made fresh and frosted with cream cheese frosting!"

– Felice Gerwitz

Fresh, Moist Apple Cake

4 cups of fresh Granny Smith apples
1 cup of chopped walnuts
1 cup of raisins
2 large or extra large eggs
½ cup of oil
1½ cups of sugar
2 tsp. vanilla extract
2 tsp. cinnamon
2 tsp. baking soda
½ tsp. salt
2 cups of flour

Peel, core and slice apples. Add ½ cup sugar and let stand, mixing with a fork from time to time. (The apple mixture can be frozen ahead of time, and will keep for about 6 months in a freezer bag. Thaw before using in the recipe.)

Mix eggs, oil, remaining 1 cup sugar, vanilla, cinnamon, salt, and baking soda. Mix well with a fork or hand mixer. Add flour. Mixture will be thick. Add apples, walnuts, and raisins.

Bake in a spring form pan, either with funnel insert or without, at 350 degrees for 45 minutes or until a tester comes out clean. (This cake tends to cook dark on top, so you may need to cover the top with foil until you have completed baking.)

Cool cake for at least 15 minutes and run a knife around the edges and bottom before removing the sides. Invert cake into a dish and cool before frosting (optional).

Cream Cheese Frosting
4 oz. cream cheese
½ stick softened butter
½ tsp. vanilla extract
2 cups powdered sugar

Mix cream cheese and butter until creamy. Add vanilla and mix. Slowly add powdered sugar 1 cup at a time and mix well until incorporated. Frost cake when cool.

Eileen Goudge

From the early days of mostly collecting rejection slips, Eileen Goudge has gone on to publish 32 novels for young adults, 13 (and still counting) of women's fiction, as well as numerous short stories and magazine articles, and one cookbook, *Something Warm from the Oven: Baking Memories, Making Memories.* Published in 1986, her first adult novel, *Garden of Lies,* spent a total of 16 weeks on *The New York Times* bestseller list. Goudge finally found true love after three failed marriages, and she was married to radio correspondent Sandy Kenyon in 1996.

PUBLISHED WORKS:

Domestic Affairs, Woman In Red, Immediate Family, Otherwise Engaged, Wish Come True, Taste Of Honey, Stranger In Paradise: A Carson Springs Novel, The Second Silence, One Last Dance, Thorns of Truth, Trail of Secrets, Blessing In Disguise and *Such Devoted Sisters*

ABOUT THE RECIPE:

"It must be my Southern heritage, as I love anything made with sweet potatoes. Marry that with cheesecake and you have a match made in heaven. I developed this recipe after reading about a bakery in Harlem that's famous for its sweet potato cheesecake. Until then, the closest I'd ever had to that was pumpkin cheesecake. So I thought, 'Why not?' I experimented and after several tries, using different crusts, came up with the following recipe, which I've since made many times. Those who've sampled it sing its praises; many have told me it's the best cheesecake they've ever tasted. It's wonderful for the holidays and a nice alternative to the standard sweet potato pie. The subtle blend of flavors and velvety texture make it a standout."

— *Eileen Goudge*

Sweet Potato Cheesecake with Praline Topping

FOR CRUST:
1¼ cup finely ground gingersnaps
¼ cup finely ground pecans
2 Tbsp. brown sugar
¼ tsp. ground ginger
5 Tbsp. unsalted butter, melted

FOR CAKE:
2 large sweet potatoes
4 8-oz. packages of cream cheese, at room temperature
1 cup firmly packed brown sugar
⅔ cup granulated sugar
5 large eggs, at room temperature
¼ cup all-purpose flour
1 tsp. cinnamon
¼ tsp. ground nutmeg
¼ tsp. ground cloves
¼ tsp. ground allspice
¼ tsp. ground mace (optional)
2 Tbsp. brandy or cognac

FOR TOPPING:
½ cup firmly packed dark brown sugar
½ cup heavy cream
¾ cup roughly chopped pecans

FOR GARNISH:
¾ cup heavy cream
¼ cup pure maple syrup

Several hours before starting the cake, wash and scrub the sweet potatoes. Make several slashes in each potato with a sharp knife, about ¼ inch deep, and place in a pan. Bake in the oven for 50 to 60 minutes, until soft when pierced with a fork. Let cool. Scoop out the soft pulp, discarding the skins. Place in a food processor and whip until smooth. Set aside 2 cups, and freeze or chill any excess for later use.

Preheat the oven to 375 degrees. Line a 9 x 13 inch baking pan with aluminum foil.

For the crust: In a small bowl, combine gingersnap crumbs, ground pecans, brown sugar, and melted butter. Press the mixture firmly over the bottom of an un-greased, 9-inch spring form pan. Bake in the oven for 12 to 15 minutes, or until lightly browned all over. Set aside to cool while the batter is prepared.

Lower the oven heat to 325 degrees.

FOR THE CAKE: In a large bowl, beat the softened cream cheese with an electric mixer at medium speed until fluffy. Combine the brown sugar and the granulated sugar, and add to the cream cheese one-fourth cup or so at a time, beating on medium speed until blended. Add the eggs, one at a time, beating on low speed just until blended after each addition.

In a separate, smaller bowl, combine the sweet potato puree, flour, and spices. Stir in the brandy.

Gradually add the sweet potato mixture to the cream cheese mixture, beating on low speed just until blended. Pour over the cooled crust in the pan, smoothing the top with a spatula.

Wrap the bottom of the pan with heavy-duty aluminum foil and nest in a larger pan, such as a roasting pan. Place on a rack in the oven and pour boiling water into the larger pan, to a depth of about two inches. Bake for about an hour and 20 minutes, until set around the edges and the center jiggles only slightly when the pan is gently shaken. Leave in the oven with the heat turned off and the oven door propped open several inches (I use a folded-over oven mitt as a wedge) for 45 minutes.

Remove the pans from the oven. Lift the spring form pan out of the larger pan and run a sharp, thin-bladed knife around the edges, as the cake will contract as it cools. Set on a wire rack to cool.

When room temperature, cover the cake loosely (still in the pan) with aluminum foil and chill in the refrigerator overnight. The following day, prepare the topping.

FOR THE TOPPING: In a small saucepan, place the brown sugar and cream. Cook over medium heat, stirring continuously until the sugar is dissolved. Simmer over low heat for about 5 minutes, until it is thickened to the consistency of hot fudge sauce. Remove from the heat. Stir in the chopped pecans and pour over the cake. Quickly spread the topping evenly over the top. Return the cake to the refrigerator until the topping is set.

Just before serving, remove the sides of the pan. Place on a serving platter, and serve with maple whipped cream, if desired.

FOR THE GARNISH: In a medium bowl, whip the cream on high speed until stiff peaks form. Drizzle in maple syrup, beating continuously on low speed, just until blended.

Dan Greenburg

Dan Greenburg's 72 books have been published in 23 countries. He writes four series of children's books: *Secrets of Dripping Fang*, *Weird Planet*, *Maximum Boy*, and *The Zack Files*. A new children's novel, *Claws*, was recently published. His bestsellers for grown-ups include *How to be a Jewish Mother*, *How to Make Yourself Miserable*, *Love Kills*, *Exes*, and *How to Avoid Love and Marriage*. The internationally recognized humorist has also written many movies and TV shows.

To research his writing, Dan has done lots of exciting things: He rode with New York firefighters for four months, running into burning buildings and overcoming a childhood fear of fire. He rode with New York homicide cops for eight months, participating in car chases and helping to capture armed killers. He flew upside down over the Pacific Ocean with a stunt pilot in an open-cockpit plane. He went to a tiger ranch in Texas, where he fed and walked Bengal tigers on leashes, and learned to discipline them by yelling "NO" and smacking them on the nose.

Dan was born and raised in Chicago, got his BFA from the University of Illinois and his MFA from UCLA. He and his wife Judith have homes in the U.S. and Canada.

ABOUT THE RECIPE:

"Before I got married, Chef Boy-ar-dee® canned cheese ravioli was the only thing I knew how to cook. It was what I cooked for myself when I was stranded at home for lunch; it was what I was forced to cook for every meal during weeklong blizzards when the snowdrifts were too high to permit leaving my apartment building. And, it was what unwary guests were served when they were foolhardy enough to come to my bachelor digs for dinner. (Few ever came a second time.)

I've been married to three quite different women, although all three were writers and all three were marvelous cooks. My current wife, Judith, who is the best wife by far, is also the best cook. We have now been together for fifteen years, so it looks as though it will last. Her cooking is so spectacular, it would be foolish for me to try and compete with her.

For the culinarily challenged, and for those trapped in week-long blizzards, here is my recipe for Chef Boy-ar-dee cheese ravioli."

– Dan Greenburg

Cheese Ravioli

1 can Chef Boy-ar-dee cheese ravioli in sauce
1 can opener, either electric or manual
1 gas or electric range
1 large saucepan
1 large spoon
1 large plate or bowl
1 potholder or equivalent

Place the can of ravioli in a can opener. If the electric variety is used, opening operation will be considerably hastened by pre-plugging into standard AC wall outlet. If a manual variety is preferred, gently squeeze handles together until you hear a soft popping sound. Then, gently but firmly turn revolving crank in a clockwise direction until the lid of the tin is almost – but not quite – separated from the body of the can.

Preheat your large saucepan under a low flame. Briskly fold contents of can into saucepan, stirring with your large spoon to taste. A covered saucepan will heat more readily than an uncovered one. A watched kettle, however, will not boil.

While ravioli is simmering, take out a clean bowl or plate and hold it in readiness. It does not pay to take out your bowl either too soon or too late. Too soon, and you risk cluttering up your work area with unnecessary utensils. Too late, and you risk pouring steaming ravioli onto your counter.

When ravioli is thoroughly heated, remove saucepan from flame, grasping handle with a potholder, baking mitt, or asbestos welder's glove. Pour content of saucepan into preset bowl or plate until saucepan is empty.

Garnish with spoon, fork, knife, and napkin.

Serves 2 normal adults, 4 children, or 1 pig.

Source: *Meatless Cooking: Celebrity Style* by Janet Barkas, Grove Press

Vivian Greene

When Vivian Greene asserts everything in life is a gift, it's not out of naiveté. The creator of Kisses®, a popular syndicated comic strip and books, has maintained an appreciative spirit while moving through a great deal of loss in her life. She lost long-time love Toby Stone to cancer. She lost 18 years' worth of work when Hurricane Andrew hit her Florida headquarters. And, she lost virtually all of her remaining possessions in shipping them to Hawaii. Her response? "I'm infinitely resilient. I have so much love in my life. Unconditional love is all that really matters."

Not that it has been easy. She has a blessing to show for each loss. Greene, who launched her cartoon character Kisses in 1971, used what she learned from Stone's life and death to write *Good Mourning*, a book on grieving, followed recently with *Mourning Glory*.

When Hurricane Andrew wiped out the business that had put her into the million-aire ranks by the age of 26, she saw it as an opportunity to head in another direction. "I said, 'I'm just going to go to Hawaii to do this.'" And the personal property loss has given her new insight into the generosity of others around her.

"The kindness I receive is just absolutely priceless," acknowledges Greene. "What I've really learned is nobody can take away what's really mine. My favorite recipe, like

Rotunda's, is sharing the laughter and love and the theme of Kisses, whose eyes are covered because *All that is real is seen with the heart.'"*

ABOUT THE RECIPE:

"My favorite recipe is a recipe for success. It all began with cookies. Rotunda, the main character in my Kisses cards and comic strip loves cookies. She is the president of Weight Wishers, and has a secret to dieting worthy of Oprah's highest award. Even if all Rotunda's diets don't work, she looks the same after 30 years."

– Vivian Greene

Rotunda's philosophy is if you eat something you really, really love, you get so excited you burn up all the calories.

Stir up a fortune!

Rotunda put her photo on the refrigerator door as a Diet Reminder. And every time she opened the refrigerator she smiled, even if she didn't diet – because she looked so happy in the picture.

"You are what you eat," her brother warned her.

"Oh," blushed Rotunda, "You mean I'm your little cookie?"

Brenda Z Guiberson

As writer, and sometimes illustrator of numerous books for children, Brenda Z Guiberson has authored several outstanding titles including: *The Emperor Lays an Egg, Into the Sea, Rain, Rain, Rain Forest, Mummy Mysteries, Mud City: A Flamingo Story*, and bestsellers *Cactus Hotel* and *Spoonbill Swamp*. *Kirkus* describes her as "one of the best science writers around for young readers." Awards have come from *School Library Journal, Booklist*, National Science Teachers, Animal Behavior Society, Bank Street College of Education, American Booksellers, Parent's Choice and others. Upcoming books include: *Ice Bears, Boreal Forest* and *Disasters*.

ABOUT THE RECIPE:

"Some authors, like me, don't write everyday. But when the words are ready to flow, I keep going on a supply of good food that can be eaten with little interruption. Here's one of my favorites."

– *Brenda Z Guiberson*

Writer's Almost Nonstop Soup

Get out a BIG soup pot.
Include any or all of the following items cut into small pieces.
Lean beef or chicken chunks browned in olive oil with garlic or onion.
Add a large can of diced tomatoes.
Add chicken, beef, or vegetable stock.
Add diced turnip, rutabaga, and potato.
Add corn, peas, green beans, and carrots.
Add black or kidney beans and black-eye peas.
Add barley or brown rice.
Add Brussels sprouts, greens, and celery.

Let the pot simmer on low while you write.

After two hours, enjoy a hot bowl of soup when you need a writing break.

Write more, eat more. Stretch, write, eat, exercise.

If you are still writing and the pot gets low, add more tomatoes, stock, or whatever you have on hand. Enjoy.

Serves one to many

Gemma Halliday

In her previous life, Gemma worked in such diverse jobs as a film actress, a teddy bear importer, a department store administrator, a preschool teacher, a temporary tattoo artist, and a 900 number psychic before finding her niche in fiction. Gemma's first book, *Spying in High Heels*, was published in 2006, and since then she has been the recipient of numerous literary awards, including the National Reader's Choice Award and two RITA Award nominations. Learn more about Gemma and her brand of humorous, off-beat mysteries at www.gemmahalliday.com.

PUBLISHED WORKS:

Spying in High Heels, Killer in High Heels, Undercover in High Heels, Alibi in High Heels, Mayhem in High Heels, These Boots Were Made for Strutting, Dreams & Desires Anthology Vol. 1 and *Vol. 2.*

ABOUT THE RECIPE:

"Having been raised in sunny California, there is nothing I love more than an afternoon by the pool with a spicy snack and a cool drink. Unfortunately, like the main character in my High Heels books, Maddie Springer, I'm much more skilled at using a credit card than a Cuisinart. The domestic arts are ones this gal has yet to master. But, inspired by Maddie's hot Latino boyfriend, I have perfected one tasty poolside specialty that always leaves my girlfriends clamoring for more – my 'Good Time Guacamole' and 'Muy Buena Margaritas.' I hope you enjoy this fun way of bringing a little California sunshine into your kitchen."

– Gemma Halliday

Good Time Guacamole

2 ripe avocados
1 tomato, seeded and chopped
½ onion chopped
2 jalapeño peppers, seeded and chopped
3 Tbsp. fresh chopped cilantro leaves
2 tsp. garlic powder
Salt and pepper to taste
2 limes
Tortilla chips

Chop the avocados in half, remove pits, and scoop the insides of the avocado into a small bowl. Add the tomato, onion, jalapeño peppers, and cilantro, being careful to wash your hands after handling the peppers, as jalapeño juice can sting your skin and eyes! Stir in garlic powder, salt and pepper. Slice the limes in half and squeeze juice over the guacamole. Serve with tortilla chips, or, for a low-fat alternative, flaky pita chips.

Muy Buena Margaritas
Cracked ice
Tequila
Grand Marnier
Lime juice
Coarse salt

In a shaker (or blender if you prefer a frostier drink) add the cracked ice, 2 parts tequila, 1 part Grand Marnier, and 1 part limejuice. Shake thoroughly, letting the ice melt a bit. Take a clean glass and rub lime juice on the rim. Pour your salt onto a plate, and dip the glass upside down in the salt, making sure it covers the wet rim. Fill the glass with ice. Then, pour in your margarita. Garnish with a slice of lime and enjoy!

Phil "The Poker Guy" Hellmuth

Phil Hellmuth's stated career goal is to become the best poker player of all time. With 11 World Series of Poker victories and more than 50 tournament titles, Hellmuth is well on his way to cementing his poker legacy, one that began shortly after his graduation from the University of Wisconsin. In fact, his laundry list of achievements in 1989 began at the tender age of 24 with his first World Series of Poker title, the youngest person to ever accomplish such a feat. He has since amassed dozens of major tournament wins internationally, including wins at The World's Biggest Seven-card Stud Tournament in Austria and Late Night Poker in Great Britain.

But his stardom doesn't stop there. The married, father of two, released his third book on playing poker, *Texas-Hold'em* in 2005. His second book *Bad Beats and Lucky Draws* was released in 2004, after his first book, *Play Poker Like the Pros*, soared to bestselling status and made *The New York Times* bestseller list. *Play Poker Like the Pros* has been translated into French and Czech. His autobiography, *Poker Brat,* is in the works.

ABOUT THE RECIPE:

"This is one of my all-time favorites from my student days at the University of Wisconsin. It tastes as good now as I remember it did, then. Serve and enjoy!"

— *Phil Hellmuth*

Phil Hellmuth's College Recipe

1 can of corn
1 lb. of ground round beef
1 - 2 cans of tomato soup
1 bag of plain macaroni noodles

Simultaneously: boil the macaroni noodles in salted water until they are done following the instructions on the bag; and brown the ground beef in a frying pan on a stove top, mixing it vigorously as it turns brown.

Then, drain the grease from the pan and drain the water from the noodles.

Then, mix in the can(s) of tomato soup with the beef – still in the frying pan.

Then, in a separate bigger serving dish, add the beef/tomato mixture, the corn, and the noodles, and mix vigorously.

Carolyn Hennesy

A Los Angeles native, Carolyn Hennesy has been in more than 100 theatrical productions spanning the Los Angeles regional and international theatre scenes. Trained at American Conservatory Theatre and the Royal Academy of Dramatic Art in London, as well as earning a dramatic scholarship to the California State University at Northridge, she has played such distinguished houses as the Mark Taper Forum, Arizona Theatre Company, Odyssey Theatre, Lobero Theatre and Geary Stage. Television work includes many regular, guest star and recurring roles in everything from episodic series to sit-coms. She can now be regularly seen on ABC's daytime drama "General Hospital" in the role of Diane Miller – Port Charles' smart and sassy mob lawyer. In addition to a full-time acting career, Carolyn is also an accomplished author, proud shop-a-holic, unabashed foodie, who teaches improvisational comedy, speaks American Sign Language and studies the flying trapeze. But more important than any of this, she is the fabulously happy new wife of actor Donald Agnelli.

PUBLISHED WORKS:

Pandora Gets Vain, Pandora Gets Jealous, Pandora Gets Lazy and *Pandora's Ancient World Recipes* with Sara Schedeen.

ABOUT THE RECIPE:

"I love this recipe because not only is it 'dee-licious' (as one of my characters, Alcie, would say), but because I can truly see this dish as being something that Sabina, the wonderful ex-Fate servant in the House of Prometheus, would make. Now, where in ancient Greece Sabina would get soy sauce, I'm not quite sure...but Sabina did serve for a time preparing food for Zeus and the other immortals on Mount Olympus. So, something tells me that she could easily have a special source for exotic ingredients...maybe Hermes, the Messenger of the Gods, procures it for her so that his friend Prometheus can enjoy this fabulously tasty lamb dish."

– Carolyn Hennesy

Sabina's Herbed Lamb Roast

Plan on 8-10 ounces of lamb per person, boneless.

2 bunches of fresh peppermint, chopped well, with no long stems
2 bunches fresh cilantro, chopped well, no long stems
Fresh juice of two lemons
¼ cup soy sauce
1 whole head of garlic, all cloves ground in a mortar and pestle with
   olive oil
¼ cup olive oil
1 Tbsp. cracked pepper

Toss all ingredients in a bowl, as the mixture should be very wet!

Lay open butterflied leg(s) of lamb. (Note: "butterflied" is the term for removing the meat from the leg bone. The butcher can do this for you or you can carefully remove meat with a boning knife with one incision down the bone and gently cutting away closely all around the bone.) The lamb will lay out in a large, flat piece with large lobes appearing to be hills and valleys of meat. Cut incisions...one or two in each lobe, leaving the inside meat exposed. Do not cut all the way through the skin.

Place lamb in a large roasting pan, fat side down. Slather generously with garlic/herb mixture over entire surface and all small crevices. Allow to marinate at least 2 hours...24 are best...anywhere in between is fine. Roast lamb under broiler 15-25 minutes. Top points should be charred and interior pink for most people. Allow to rest for 10 minutes, before carving. Slice thinly and drizzle *jus* over meat before going to the table.

Source: *Pandora's Ancient World Recipes,* Authors: Carolyn Hennesy and Sara Schedeen.

Cliff & Nancy Hollenbeck

Cliff and Nancy Hollenbeck are world travelers, leading authors, photographers and filmmakers, specializing in image-making for major airlines, cruise lines, resorts, publishers, tourism associations, advertising agencies and national tourist boards. They have authored more than two dozen books on travel, photography and business, including bestselling pictorials on Hawaii and the Mexican Riviera. They also authored the book *Mexico* with renowned novelist James A. Michener. Cliff has twice been named Travel Photographer of the Year. He wrote the travel-mystery novel *Acapulco Goodbye* and has composed and produced Italian arias. The Hollenbecks' film company has received Gold Medals at the International Film Festivals in New York and Chicago, and several TELLYs for television videos. They reside in Seattle, Washington.

ABOUT THE RECIPE:

"The wonderful dish 'Sugo alla Puttanesca' originated in 1950s Naples, Italy. Ladies of the evening used its fragrant aroma and spicy taste as advertising to attract sailors on liberty from visiting fleets. Today's recipes for this 'bad girls' pasta' vary by family, restaurant and region, depending on the odds and ends in the pantry and what is fresh from the garden. Over the years, the Hollenbeck family has made this pasta as a robust spaghetti ragù, revising the original ingredients with each generation's taste for travel and flavor."

Puttanesca Ragù makes a wonderful side dish to a lean steak. We enjoy a hearty *Amarone* wine, salt-free Tuscan bread and a small *misto* salad to complete the meal. Enjoy!"

– Cliff and Nancy Hollenbeck

Puttanesca Ragù

½ cup extra virgin olive oil
2 cups yellow onions, chopped
2 cups fresh tomatoes, chopped and drained
2 cups mushrooms, sliced thick
4 cloves garlic, chopped fine
3 Tbsp. capers
¼ tsp. dried pepperoncino chili flakes
¼ cup fresh basil, shredded
2 cups tomato sauce (or favorite red pasta sauce)
1 cup anchovy-stuffed green olives
1 lb. ground wild boar (or lean hamburger)
2 Tbsp. balsamic vinegar
Pecorino cheese for topping

Warm the olive oil in a large stainless steel or non-stick pan over medium heat. Sauté the onions, stirring or tossing frequently until transparent. Reduce to medium-low heat and add mushrooms and continue the sauté.

At the same time, sauté the meat in a separate pan until completely cooked. Drain and add to the sauce after the mushrooms have begun to change color.

Add the tomatoes and tomato sauce, stir, and bring to a soft boil. Then add olives, capers, basil, chili flakes, garlic and balsamic vinegar.

While the sauce is simmering, boil one pound of spaghetti or linguini pasta until medium soft. Do not add any oil or salt. When the pasta is done, drain the water and return to the pot. Gently stir in the finished *Puttanesca Ragù*. Shave several leaves of Pecorino cheese on top of each serving.

Serves 6

Amy Houts

Although Amy Houts now lives in the rural northwest Missouri town of Maryville, she was born in New York. She has lived in several states including Maryland, Kansas, Tennessee, and Mississippi. After staying home with her children, Amy went back to college and earned a degree in Library Science. She has worked as a children's librarian, preschool teacher, features writer for the local newspaper, and she currently freelances. She is the author of 24 books and three cookbooks, and instructs more than 100 students in a correspondence course on writing for children.

Amy's interest in cooking began at an early age. She was encouraged to cook as a teenager and often made the family meals. After high school, her love of cooking and baking led her to attend the Culinary Institute of America in Hyde Park, New York. She worked in a restaurant for a year and enjoys cooking for her family and friends, as well as writing about food.

She and her husband, Steve, a seventh grade science teacher, have two grown daughters. Amy spends her days mostly at home, writing and teaching, in the company of her adorable boxer-mix dog, Pepper.

PUBLISHED WORKS:

Dora the Explorer: Preschool Adventure, Dora the Explorer: Addition, Dora the Explorer: Subtraction, Dora the Explorer: Safety, Dora the Explorer: Trace & Draw, Winifred Witch and her Very Own Cat, Cooking Around the Calendar with Kids and *On the Farm.*

ABOUT THE RECIPE:

"This recipe for rolls is one I've been making for more than three decades. What I love about it is not only the taste and texture but also the convenience of being able to make the dough days ahead and storing it in the refrigerator. That way, I can take out just as much dough as I need to have fresh rolls. Traditionally, I make these for Thanksgiving or other special occasions."

– Amy Houts

Company Refrigerator Rolls

$\frac{1}{2}$ cup warm water
1 package (2$\frac{1}{2}$ tsp.) yeast
1 tsp. sugar
1 cup milk
$\frac{1}{3}$ cup butter or margarine
6 Tbsp. sugar
2 tsp. salt
1 egg or 2 egg whites
5-5$\frac{1}{2}$ cups unbleached white flour

Pour the water into a small bowl. Test a drop on your wrist to see if it is just warm, not hot. Children can add the yeast, 1 tsp. sugar, and stir. Set aside. Children can help measure and pour milk, butter or margarine, sugar and salt into a saucepan. Heat just until butter or margarine melts. Remove from heat and let cool to lukewarm.

Pour milk mixture into a large bowl. Add softened yeast mixture. Children can add the egg or egg whites, and the 2$\frac{1}{2}$ cups flour. Stir with a wooden spoon until smooth. Give everyone a turn. Continue adding enough flour to make a soft dough. You might need to stir, if it gets too difficult for the children.

Let the dough rest for 10 minutes.

Then knead the dough on a floured board or cloth, by folding $\frac{1}{3}$ of the dough towards you, pushing and turning. Children will enjoy punching, pressing, and palming dough. Use enough flour to keep it from getting sticky. Continue kneading for about 10 minutes.

Place dough in greased bowl and cover, or use a large (gallon-size) plastic bag. Zip or use twister tie, leaving enough room in the bag for dough to rise. Place in refrigerator overnight.

Shape rolls by cutting dough into 24 to 30 pieces. Children can shape into a ball or into a "snake" and then a knot, figure eight, braid or other shape.

Place on a greased cookie sheet. Cover with a dishtowel; let rise 2-3 hours until almost doubled in bulk.

Bake in 375 degree oven for 15 minutes or until golden brown.

Yield: about 2-dozen rolls

Source: *Cooking Around the Calendar with Kids* by Amy Houts

J. A. Jance

As a second-grader in Mrs. Spangler's Greenway School class, Judy Jance was introduced to Frank Baum's *Wizard of Oz* series. Immediately she was hooked and knew, from that moment on, that she wanted to be a writer. Jance was the third child in a large family in southeastern Arizona. This left her alone in a crowd and helped her become an introspective reader and a top student. When she graduated from Bisbee High School, she received an academic scholarship that made her the first person in her family to attend a four-year college. She graduated with a degree in English and Secondary Ed.; later she received her M. Ed. in Library Science. Jance taught high school at Tucson's Pueblo High School and was a librarian at Indian Oasis School District in Sells, Arizona.

ABOUT THE RECIPE:

"The first book I wrote, a slightly fictionalized version of a series of murders that happened in Tucson, was never published. For one thing, it was twelve hundred pages long. My agent finally sat me down and told me that she thought I was a better writer of fiction than I was of non-fiction. Why, she suggested, didn't I try my hand at a novel?

The result of that conversation was the first Detective Beaumont book, *Until Proven Guilty*. Since 1985, when that was published, there have been fourteen more Beau books. My work also includes eight Joanna Brady books set where I grew up. In addition there are two thrillers, *Hour of the Hunter* and *Kiss of the Bees,* that reflect what I learned during my years teaching on the Tohono O'Odham reservation west of Tucson. The Sugarloaf Café Sweet Rolls recipe is featured in the Ali Reynolds book series."

– J. A. Jance

Sugarloaf Café Sweet Rolls
(As featured in the Ali Reynolds series)

Dough:
4³/₄ cups all-purpose flour; plus ²/₃ cup all-purpose flour (held separate)
1 cup warm water
1 packet instant yeast
1 large egg + 1 yolk (reserve remaining egg white)
¹/₂ cup sugar
1 tsp. Kosher salt
Pinch of fresh-grated nutmeg
¹/₂ cup sour cream (whole)

Filling:
1¹/₂ cup dark brown sugar
1 Tbsp. corn syrup
3 Tbsp. softened (unsalted) butter
6 oz. chopped pecans
¹/₂ tsp. ground cinnamon
Pinch of fresh-grated nutmeg

Icing:
8 oz. softened cream cheese
¹/₂ cup sugar
¹/₃ cup heavy cream
Optional: orange zest

In a large mixing bowl, sift together 4³/₄ cups flour with the nutmeg, then add in the sugar, salt, and yeast. Mix in the egg, egg yolk and water, and knead for about 5 to 8 minutes, or until dough just turns into a smooth, elastic ball.

Work in sour cream and additional ²/₃ cups flour, and knead until dough takes up the additional ingredients. The dough should be slightly wet and a little sticky.

Place in a lightly buttered bowl, cover and set in a warm spot until dough has doubled in bulk.

While dough is rising, prepare the filling by mixing together the dark brown sugar, nutmeg, cinnamon, corn syrup and softened butter until uniform. Then, add in the chopped pecans.

When dough has doubled in bulk, punch down, and roll out on a lightly floured surface to a rectangle approximately 17" long x 14" wide x $1/8$" thick. Evenly distribute the filling, leaving approximately 1" at the top without filling; brush this edge with remaining egg white.

Roll up into a 17" long log and allow to rest on seam for a few minutes to ensure a good seal. Using a large, sharp knife, gently trim the ends of the log and discard, then cut into 8 equal sections of approximately 2".

Prepare two 8" x 8" x 2" cake pans, by coating the interior lightly with softened butter, and dusting with flour.

Place rolls upright (4 rolls per pan), allowing equal space between rolls and the sidewall of the pan. Preheat oven to 325 degrees; Cover lightly with either parchment paper or loose plastic wrap and allow to rise until they begin to touch, almost doubling in width*. Bake for 35 to 40 minutes, until just golden on top.

While rolls are baking, prepare the icing by creaming together (room temperature) cream cheese and sugar. Add in $1/3$ cup heavy cream and mix on medium speed for 2 to 3 minutes. Spread on tops of rolls immediately after removing from oven.

Makes 8 large rolls

*After covering, you can also place these in the refrigerator and allow them to sit overnight. Let them come up to room temperature before baking in the morning.

©Thomas Schilb, November 25, 2006

Stephanie Kallos

Photo by Susan Doupz

Stephanie Kallos spent 20 years in the theatre as an actress and teacher. A graduate of the University of Washington's Professional Actor Training Program, she was privileged to work with many regional theatres, including the Illinois, Idaho, and Georgia Shakespeare Festivals. Her short fiction has earned a Raymond Carver Award and a Pushcart Prize nomination. *Broken for You,* Stephanie's first novel, received the Washington State Book Award, was nominated for a Quills Award in the Best Debut Author category, and was chosen by Sue Monk Kidd as the December 2004 book club selection for NBC's Today Show. Her second novel, *Sing Them Home,* was published in January 2008. A Midwest native, Stephanie now lives with her husband and sons in Seattle.

ABOUT THE RECIPE:

"For me the most wonderful meals are the simplest, such as those revolving around a bowl of good soup and a glass of wine. I made this recipe for the first time when I was a junior at the University of Nebraska and had been invited to a "progressive" Thanksgiving dinner organized by our theatre department chairman, Rex McGraw. Rex asked several students to host different courses (naturally, I volunteered to be the soup course) and we spent the holiday leisurely traveling from one student's home to another. We ended the day (and the feast) at Rex's home, where he served Japanese

Plum Wine and a beautiful assortment of dessert cheeses and fruit. The whole event felt very grown-up and exotic to me, such a departure from all the previous turkey-and-pumpkin-pie Thanksgivings of my life. I'm sure it was the first time I used cumin in a recipe! So (with apologies to vegans and the lactose-intolerant), here is one of the best soup recipes I know. Thirty years later, it's still a favorite with me, and has become a favorite with my husband and children as well."

– Stephanie Kallos

Corn and Cheddar Cheese Chowder

1 large potato, peeled and diced
2 cups boiling salted water
1 bay leaf
¼ tsp. dried sage
½ tsp. powdered cumin
3 Tbsp. butter
1 onion, finely chopped
3 Tbsp. flour
1¼ cups heavy cream
Kernels from 2 ears of corn (about 2 cups, frozen works fine)
¼ tsp. nutmeg
1½ cups cheddar cheese, grated (about 4 oz.)
4-5 Tbsp. dry white wine

Garnishes as desired:
Chopped chives and/or parsley
Fine slivers of red and green pepper

Peel and dice the potato and boil it in the salted water with the bay leaf, sage, and cumin until just barely tender – 10-15 minutes.

Melt the butter in a saucepan and sauté the chopped onion in it for a while; then add the flour. Mix well and add the cream, stirring with a whisk.

Pour this sauce into the potatoes and their water, adding also the corn kernels. Add the rest of the seasonings and let the soup simmer gently for about 10 minutes.

Then stir in the grated cheese and the wine and mix well; warm until the cheese is completely melted, correct the seasonings as needed, garnish as desired, and serve.

(A variation: eliminate the corn and nutmeg and substitute beer for the wine. Top with popcorn!)

A wonderful, hearty, rich soup, recommended for cold nights and 4-6 hungry people!

Peg Kehret

Peg Kehret has published 45 books; all but two are for young people. Her books have won numerous awards, including the PEN Center Award in children's literature, Golden Kite Award from the Society of Children's Book Writers and Illustrators, Henry Bergh Award from the ASPCA, and dozens of state Young Reader awards, where students vote for their favorite book.

She volunteers for Pasado's Safe Haven and three of her books (*The Stranger Next Door*, *Spy Cat*, and *Trapped*) are co-authored by Pete the cat. Part of her royalties help support a mobile spay/neuter clinic for pets of low-income residents.

Peg has two grown children, four grandchildren, a shelter dog and two rescued cats. Visit her online at www.pegkehret.com.

PUBLISHED WORKS:

Small Steps 10th Anniversay Edition, Tell It Like It Is, Abduction, Escaping the Giant Wave, Five Pages a Day: A Writer's Journey, Don't Tell Anyone, Saving Lilly, My Brother Made Me Do It, The Hideout, Acting Natural and *Stolen Children.*

ABOUT THE RECIPE:

"My recipe for oatmeal pancakes is from my mother, who was a terrific cook. One reason it's a favorite, besides the fact that the pancakes are easy and delicious, is that my copy of the recipe is in her handwriting. Across the top she wrote, 'Good and good for you.' Each time I see that, I can hear Mother urging me to eat healthy food."

– Peg Kehret

Oatmeal Pancakes

1 cup rolled oats
½ cup whole-wheat flour
½ tsp. baking soda
1⅓ cups buttermilk
2 eggs, beaten
1 tsp. vanilla
1-2 cups blueberries (optional)

Combine oats, flour and soda. Add buttermilk, eggs and vanilla. Mix to form batter.

Fold in blueberries, if desired. (I always do, but the original recipe does not call for them.)

Drop onto hot nonstick skillet and fry on both sides.

Good served with warm maple syrup or applesauce.

Faye Kellerman

Photo ©2006 Jonathan Exley

Bestselling author Faye Kellerman created the successful Peter Decker/Rina Lazarus series of novels, as well as a thriller, *Moon Music*. Her historical novel, *The Quality of Mercy* takes a different direction. Kellerman is the proud mother of four children. She lives in Los Angeles, California and Santa Fe, New Mexico with her husband, author Jonathan Kellerman.

PUBLISHED WORKS:

The Ritual Bath, Sacred and Profane, The Quality of Mercy, Milk and Honey, Day of Atonement, False Prophet, Grievous Sin, Sanctuary, Justice, Prayers for the Dead, Serpent's Tooth, Moon Music, Jupiter's Bones, Stalker, The Forgotten, Stone Kiss, Street Dreams, Straight Into Darkness, The Garden of Eden and other Criminal Delights.

ABOUT THE RECIPE:

"My son forwarded me this recipe from the chef, Jeff Besh. Here it is with his, and my, modifications."

– Faye Kellerman

Moon Music Ribs

4 lbs. beef short ribs, cut "flanken-style" across the bone
Coarse salt and pepper
3 cups Zinfandel wine
1 Tbsp. honey
6 oz. canned, chopped tomatoes
1½ cups beef broth
1 tsp. minced garlic
1 sprig of fresh thyme
2 bay leaves
2 oz. olive oil
2 large carrots cut
2 stalks celery cut
2 large onions cut
6 whole mushrooms
2 oz. dried mushrooms – porcini preferable

1. Preheat oven to 275 degrees. Season short ribs with salt and pepper. Be generous. In a mixing bowl, whisk together Zinfandel, honey, tomatoes, beef broth, garlic thyme, bay leaves and a pinch of salt.

2. Pour olive oil into a heavy pot or Dutch oven and place over high heat. When oil is hot, working in small batches, sear the meat. Turn each piece to brown on all sides before removing from pot.

3. When all beef is browned and removed from pot, add the onions, carrots and celery. Season with salt and pepper. Add fresh mushrooms five minutes later and continue to brown for another five minutes.

4. Return beef to pot along with the wine mixture. Allow the wine to come to a boil before reducing heat, skimming the fat from the surface.

5. After simmering for several minutes, add the dry mushrooms. Cover and simmer over very low heat until meat is fork tender and nearly falling off the bone – 1½ to 2 hours. Or, bake in the oven at low heat – 275 degrees for 3 hours or until the beef is tender.

6. Once the meat is adequately soft, remove it and the vegetables from the pot and keep warm. Turn up the heat and reduce pot liquids until thickened, about ten minutes. Season with salt and pepper to taste.

7. Transfer ribs to four shallow bowls, spooning the liquid over the top.

Serves 4

Jonathan Kellerman

Photo © Jonathan Exley

Born in New York City in 1949, Jonathan Kellerman grew up in Los Angeles. Like his fictional protagonist, Alex Delaware, Jonathan received at Ph.D. in psychology at the age of 24, with a specialty in the treatment of children.

In 1985, Jonathan's first novel, *When the Bough Breaks*, was published to enormous critical and commercial success and became a *New York Times* bestseller. It also won the Edgar Allan Poe and Anthony Boucher Awards for Best First Novel and was made into a television movie. Since then, Jonathan has published a bestselling crime novel every year, and occasionally, two per year. In addition, he has written and illustrated two books for children and a nonfiction volume on childhood violence. Though no longer active as a psychotherapist, he is a Clinical Professor of Pediatrics and Psychology at University of Southern California's Keck School of Medicine.

Jonathan is married to bestselling novelist Faye Kellerman and they have four children.

PUBLISHED WORKS:

When the Bough Breaks, Blood Test, Over the Edge, The Butcher's Theater, Silent Partner, Time Bomb, Private Eyes, Devil's Waltz, Bad Love, Self-Defense, The Web, The Clinic, Survival of the Fittest, Billy Straight, Savage Spawn: Reflections on Violent Children, Monster, Dr. Death, Flesh and Blood, The Murder Book, A Cold Heart, The Conspiracy Club, Therapy, Double Homicide, Twisted, Rage, Gone, Capital Crimes and *Obsession.*

ABOUT THE RECIPE:

"I'm not much of a cook, but you can certainly use my recipe for a hybrid Manhattan cocktail."

– Jonathan Kellerman

Midtown Manhattan

1 oz. Knob Creek Bourbon
1 oz. Cognac
Dash of sweet vermouth
Dash of orange bitters

Mix in a cocktail shaker,

Pour on the rocks with a cherry

Serves one happy person

Bharti Kirchner

Bharti Kirchner is the author of four acclaimed novels including *Pastries: A Novel of Desserts and Discoveries, Darjeeling, Sharmila's Book*, and *Shiva Dancing*. Her books have been translated into many foreign languages. An award-winning cook, she is also the author of four cookbooks, including *Indian Inspired, The Healthy Cuisine of India, Vegetarian Burgers,* and *The Bold Vegetarian*. Her culinary pieces have appeared in numerous magazines such as *Food & Wine, Cooking Light* and *Vegetarian Times*. She also has a short story, Promised Tulips, to be published in the anthology of mystery stories, *Seattle Noir*.

ABOUT THE RECIPE:

"Long before fusion cooking became popular, I was combining pasta with Indian or Thai ingredients in my kitchen, with excellent results. Pasta, I found, is a foil for sauces with a kick, and thus *Thai Tortellini* was born. When *The Bold Vegetarian* was published, readers would call or write me to say how much they enjoyed that recipe and how easy it was to prepare. *Thai Tortellini* is a dish to attempt on days you long for a spicy flavor or when you wish to dazzle your dinner guests with a tasty, pretty meal."

– *Bharti Kirchner*

Thai Tortellini

1 to 1½ Tbsp. canola oil
1 cup thinly sliced onion
½ to ¾ tsp. Thai yellow curry paste
1 large red bell pepper
½ pound broccoli, cut into florets
½ to ¾ cup coconut milk, stirred to mix the thin and thick parts
    before measuring
8 oz. spinach/cheese tortellini or any tortellini
Chopped cilantro for garnish

In hot oil in large skillet, sauté onion until it is translucent, about two minutes. Add curry paste and stir until evenly distributed. Add ¼ cup water and bring to a boil. Add bell pepper and broccoli. Lower heat and simmer, covered, 5 to 7 minutes, or just until the vegetables are tender-crisp. Don't let them get too soft. Remove from heat and keep warm.

Cook tortellini according to package directions. While it is draining, add coconut milk to the vegetables in skillet and return to very low heat. (The heat is kept low to keep coconut milk from curdling.) As soon as coconut milk is mixed in with the sauce, add tortellini, and stir gently to coat with the sauce.

Garnish with cilantro.

Best served immediately. If allowed to stand, tortellini will drink up some of the sauce, reducing its volume, although the dish will still taste good.

Adapted from *The Bold Vegetarian* by Bharti Kirchner.

Jayne Ann Krentz

Photo by Sigrid Estrada

The author of more than 40 *New York Times* bestsellers, Jayne Ann Krentz writes the kind of books she has always loved best – romantic-suspense – under her own name as well as the pen names Amanda Quick and Jayne Castle.

She earned a B.A. in History from the University of California at Santa Cruz and went on to obtain a Masters degree in Library Science from San Jose State University in California. Before she began writing full time she worked as a librarian in both academic and corporate libraries.

She is married and lives with her husband, Frank, in Seattle, Washington.

PUBLISHED WORKS:

Dark Light, The Third Circle, The River Knows, Sizzle and Burn, White Lies, Silver Master, Dangerous, Desire, Eclipse Bay, The Paid Companion and *Surrender.*

ABOUT THE RECIPE:

"Summer means many things to people – flip-flops, sunglasses, tee-shirts. But to me, it means PESTO! I love the stuff and I always make my own.

The pesto that comes in jars is way too runny and way too garlicky for my taste. I've done a lot of experimenting over the years and the pesto that has evolved in my kitchen bears little resemblance to the traditional version.

My apologies to purists but, hey, I'm the one who eats it so I'm having it my way. Another note to you purists out there – you know who you are – no, I don't add any garlic. I am not a fan of garlic. But if you like garlic, I suppose it wouldn't hurt."

– Jayne Ann Krentz

Jayne's Summer Pesto

Wash and spin-dry the leaves of the following green things. You'll need enough to fill the bowl of a large food processor (lightly packed).

1 large bunch fresh basil leaves
1 large bunch fresh Italian flat leaf parsley, or arugula, or a mix of the two.

Place washed and dried green things in food processor bowl. Then add the following. (All measures are suggestions only – feel free to experiment).

$^1/_3$ cup of green olives sliced in half (just to make sure there are no pits). Yes, you can use the kind they put into martinis.

$^1/_4$ cup of toasted pine nuts. (You know how to toast pine nuts, don't you? Just toss them in a dry pan over medium heat and let them toast until golden. Hint: Shake the pan a lot. The little suckers will burn on you if you don't keep them moving.)

$^1/_3$ cup of grated Parmesan cheese or Parmesan-Reggiano blend.
Juice and zest of one lime
$^1/_2$ tsp. of hot sauce

Pulse all the above together until you get it down to the consistency that you like. I prefer my pesto with a lot of texture but some like it very smooth.

Now add some good quality OLIVE OIL, a couple of tablespoons at a time and pulse or stir some more until you get it the way you want it. Again, I prefer a thick mixture but some folks like it thin and runny. I don't know why.

Add salt to taste. Usually the olives and Parmesan add enough salt but you might want a little more. And there you have it: summer magic.

Bruce Lansky

One of the most popular children's poets in North America, Bruce Lansky has published nearly two-dozen books of funny poetry and silly songs. They have sold well over 3 million copies. He lives in Minneapolis, Minnesota where the temperature often drops below zero during too-long winters. For that reason, he enjoys visits to schools, bookstores, and libraries across the country for entertaining performances of his stand-up comedy, poetry and silly songs. Bruce's works can be found online at www.gigglepoetry.com, one of the most popular children's poetry websites. He has created several other popular websites including poetryteachers.com and fictionteachers.com for teachers, and meadowbrookpress.com for customers.

"I can't possibly visit all the schools that want me, so I try, via the Internet, to help kids discover the fun of reading and writing stories and poetry," said Lansky.

PUBLISHED WORKS:

Ten poetry anthologies, three song books, and two books of poetry: *My Dog Ate My Homework* and *If Pigs Could Fly.*

ABOUT THE RECIPE:

"On a family trip, I was sitting at the breakfast table with my still-sleepy niece, Sarah. When her mother breezed into the kitchen for a cup of coffee, the 7-year-old girl asked, 'Can I have some cereal, mom?'

I noticed that there was a box of cereal, a bowl, a spoon, and a container of milk— all thoughtfully placed on or near Sarah's place mat. I realized that Sarah wasn't wondering if her mother would give her permission to have cereal. No, Sarah was asking her mother to pour the cereal in the bowl, pour the milk into the cereal, and put the spoon into the bowl so she could pretty much eat the cereal without so much as opening her sleepy eyes.

So, the idea behind my breakfast poem is that for some kids, 'making' a bowl of cereal in the morning is a project as big for them as building a nuclear bomb would be for a North Korean scientist. In my poem, the kid takes more initiative than sleepy Sarah, but the kid in the poem is ultimately as helpless (and clueless) as Sarah and needs mom to save the day.

You'll probably notice that my breakfast poem has no rhythm or rhyme. It's a 'list poem,' which means that it's a list of stuff (in this case, "recipe instructions") that are arranged in order and written in a fairly minimalistic style. This is one of the easiest kind of poems for kids to learn to write (precisely because there's no rhythm and rhyme to worry about)."

– Bruce Lansky

How to Make Breakfast on a School Day

1. Grab cereal box from pantry.
2. Rip open box top. (If bunny, bear, or smiling athlete is upside down, turn box over and open other box top.)
3. Pull plastic inner-bag out of box.
4. Using sharp knife, stab bag to make on opening through which you can pour cereal into bowl.
5. If cereal winds up on kitchen floor, call dog (to eat cereal off floor – before your mother sees it.)
6. Tell mother you don't "feel like" dry cereal.
7. Mention that preparing breakfast has caused you to miss school bus.
8. Ask mother to drive you to school – and stop at McDonald's for an Egg McMuffin® on the way.

Serves one

Julie Larios

Julie Larios is a poet who publishes work for children and adults. For five years, she was the poetry editor for *The Cortland Review*, and her poetry has been published by *The Atlantic Monthly, McSweeney's, Swink, The Georgia Review, Ploughshares, The Threepenny Review, Field,* and others. Recipient of an Academy of American Poets Prize and the Pushcart Prize for Poetry, Julie's work has been chosen twice for *The Best American Poetry* series. Her latest book of poetry for children, *The Yellow Elephant*, was named a *Boston Globe*-Horn Book Honor Book in 2006. Julie lives in Seattle.

ABOUT THE RECIPE:

"This recipe first appeared in a book of family recipes gathered by my good friend (and children's author) Laura Kvasnosky. Laura was sweet enough to give me a copy, and I now find some of my favorite recipes (and stories) within its pages. Someday I hope to gather the same kind of book together for my own family – Laura's book includes recipes, genealogical family trees, vintage photographs and anecdotal family history. I've adapted the recipe a bit in the years since I first gave it a try and it's become a great family favorite at our house. Enjoy!"

– Julie Larios

Chicken Almondrata

3 cloves of garlic, finely chopped
½ onion, chopped
3 Tbsp. olive oil
2 Tbsp. butter
6 chicken breasts, cubed
1 bottle salsa Verde (you can mix an 8 oz. can of hot green sauce
    with a small bottle of mild green sauce, or go with all hot if you
    like things spicy)
1 pint cream (you can substitute half and half, but then add some
    time reducing to sauce consistency)
8-12 flour tortillas
3 cups Monterey Jack cheese (we've also experimented with ranchero,
    pepper jack, Swiss…)
1 cup of almonds, finely chopped
Handful of crumbled Cojita cheese (optional)

Sauté the garlic and onions in oil until transparent and remove to a bowl. Sauté the chicken in the same oil for several minutes, until cooked through. Remove from heat and mix with onions and garlic. In a separate frying pan, heat one flour tortilla at a time in a very small amount of melted butter until heated through and slightly bubbly. Put a little chicken and grated cheese in each tortilla and roll, then place in a shallow oven-safe backing dish. Repeat until dish is filled.

Bake at 300 degrees for 20 minutes, or until cheese is thoroughly melted and tortillas begin to crisp slightly. Meanwhile, heat salsa, nuts and cream on stove top, reducing to a good sauce consistency.

To serve, pour sauce over the filled tortilla, then sprinkle the leftover cheese on top (or if you feel adventurous, sprinkle Cojita cheese on top – it crumbles well and has a salty/ sharp taste. Looks good on top, too!) Make sure everyone gets plenty of the sauce!

Serves 4 to 6

Nancy Leson

The Seattle Times food columnist and radio food commentator for NPR-affiliate KPLU, Nancy Leson serves up a bounty of information and culinary tips on Pacific Northwest food, cooking, dining and restaurants. She spent nearly 20 years waiting tables before trading her apron and corkscrew for a writer's notebook and keyboard. A native Philadelphian, Nancy joined *The Seattle Time*s as lead restaurant critic in 1998 and today keeps her finger on the pulse of the local food scene on her blog, All You Can Eat (www.seattletimes.com/allyoucaneat). She lives with her husband and son in Edmonds, Washington.

PUBLISHED WORKS:

Seattle Best Places 7th Edition, Editor; *Northwest Budget Traveler: Cheap Eats, Cheap Sleeps, Affordable Adventure,* Editor; *Zagat Survey,* Seattle/Pacific Northwest.

ABOUT THE RECIPE:

"A decade ago, shortly after my son was born, I became the staff restaurant critic and columnist for *The Seattle Times.* Soon after, I had the great good fortune to meet Vijay Niles – who operated a daycare center in a home perfumed with the exotic scent of Sri Lankan foods. Vijay was a godsend: not only because she was the most warm and caring daycare provider a crazy-busy mom could ask for, but because she was an amazing cook and always generous with her deliciousities (curries! chutneys! vadas! idlis!). She even taught me how to make her justly 'famous' beef curry – a recipe I've long since adopted as my own."

– Nancy Leson

Sri Lankan Beef Curry

3 pounds chuck roast, trimmed of excess fat and cut into small chunks
7 cloves garlic, peeled and smashed
Fresh gingerroot (a quarter-sized slice)
¾ tsp. turmeric, divided
5 green cardamom pods, lightly smashed
1 cinnamon stick, broken in half
1 tsp. salt, divided
1 Tbsp. vegetable oil
⅛ tsp. black mustard seed
¼ tsp. fennel seed
¼ tsp. fenugreek seed
6 fresh curry leaves
2 fresh Thai (bird) chilies
1 medium onion, diced
1 Tbsp. ground coriander
1 Tbsp. chili powder
1 Tbsp. curry powder
1 large tomato, diced
½ fresh lime, juiced
2 Tbsp. milk
Hot cooked rice

1. Prepare beef and set aside. Using a blender or food processor, pulse garlic and ginger until you have a rough paste. In a large bowl, mix the paste with ½ teaspoon turmeric, cardamom, cinnamon and ½ teaspoon salt. Add beef, mixing until thoroughly coated.

2. In a large, heavy-bottomed pot, heat oil over medium-low heat then, add mustard, fennel and fenugreek seeds, curry leaves and chilies. When leaves begin to puff, add onion and sauté until golden brown, about 10 minutes.

3. Add beef to onion mixture, stirring well. Then, add enough water to just cover and cook over high heat for five minutes. Lower heat to medium-low and cook 30 minutes more. Strain the water from the meat, reserving the broth.

4. Add coriander, chili powder, curry powder, ¼ teaspoon turmeric and ½ teaspoon salt to cooked beef and mix thoroughly. Add tomato and cook over low heat, covered, for 10 minutes.

5. Add reserved meat and approximately half of the broth to the pot and cook, covered, for about 40 minutes or until the curry sauce has reduced and thickened substantially. Add the reserved broth, if needed. Uncover the pot toward the end of the cooking time. Stir in lime juice, then milk. Serve over rice.

Makes 4 servings

Note: Spices used in this recipe are readily available at Indian markets and at other Asian and/or specialty markets throughout Greater Seattle or online. Though they add much flavor, curry leaves may be omitted, and the fresh leaves may be dried and stored for future use.

Lisa Lillien

Lisa Lillien is a "foodologist" and the founder of Hungry-Girl.com. More than half a million people devour Lisa's tips and tricks every Monday through Friday. Her first book, *Hungry Girl: Recipes and Survival Strategies for Guilt-Free Eating in the Real World* was released in 2002 and debuted at #2 on *The New York Times* bestseller list. *Hungry Girl: 200 Under 200 – 200 Recipes Under 200 Calories* will be available in 2009.

ABOUT THE RECIPE

"This recipe for Lord of the Onion Rings was created in 2006 and was the first 'Hungry Girl' recipe to utilize my now-famous Fiber One® 'faux frying' technique. Pulverizing Fiber One Original Bran Cereal in a blender is a great way to make high-fiber, low-calorie 'breadcrumbs' that can also be used to coat chicken, shrimp, zucchini and more."

– Lisa Lillien

Lord of the Onion Rings

1 large onion
½ cup Fiber One® bran cereal (original)
¼ cup fat-free liquid egg substitute
Dash of salt
Optional: Additional salt, black pepper, oregano, garlic powder,
    onion powder, etc.

Preheat oven to 375 degrees.

1. Cut the ends off of the onion and remove the outer layer. Cut onion into ½-inch-wide slices, and separate into individual rings.

2. Using a blender or food processor, grind the cereal to a breadcrumb-like consistency. Pour crumbs into a small dish and mix in salt, and any optional spices you like.

3. Fill a small bowl (just large enough for onion rings to fit in) with egg substitute. One by one, coat each ring first in egg and then in the "breadcrumbs." Give each ring a shake after the egg bath.

4. Evenly place rings on a baking dish coated with nonstick spray. Bake for 20 to 25 minutes, flipping rings over about halfway through.

Makes one humongous serving.

Mark Lindquist

A native of the Pacific Northwest, Mark Lindquist attended the University of Washington. He then transferred to the University of Southern California at Los Angeles. After graduating, he secured a position as a copywriter for a Hollywood movie studio. His first novel, *Sad Movies,* was based on this personal experience. Two more novels followed: *Carnival Desires* chronicled his Hollywood experience, and *Never Mind Nirvana* is an inside-view of late-nineties Seattle. He is also the author of screenplays, book reviews and articles for major publications.

In 2004, Mark became the trial-team chief of the drug unit for the Prosecuting Attorney in Pierce County, Washington. There, he focused on aggressively prosecuting illegal methamphetamine labs. Since that time, meth labs have been reduced by approximately 80 percent in Pierce County. Mark was also one of the attorneys who successfully prosecuted the notorious Tacoma Mall shooter, Dominick Maldonado. Mark lives in Tacoma, Washington. His fourth novel, *The King of Methlehem,* was published in 2007.

ABOUT THE RECIPE:

"This one is easy and tastes great after a long day in court. Put up your feet and sip."

– Mark Lindquist

Tolstoy Alexander
(modified Brandy Alexander)

1 shot of crème de cacao
1 shot of heavy cream
1 shot of brandy
1 shot of vodka

Mix in shaker half-filled with ice cubes, strain into martini or lowball glass, add fresh-ground nutmeg. You can substitute for dessert, or even dinner.

Serves one tired prosecutor

Portia Little

Photo by Dede Hatch Photography

A prolific writer, Portia Little has been a food columnist, feature writer, author and editor for magazines, newspapers, universities, and financial institutions. She is a Syracuse University graduate and resides on the Rhode Island shore.

PUBLISHED WORKS:

The Easy Vegetarian, New England Seashore Recipes & Rhyme, Lusty Limericks & Luscious Desserts and *Bread Pudding Bliss*.

ABOUT THE RECIPE:

"I love to be creative when making bread puddings, adding whatever is on my shelf crying out: 'Make me into bread pudding!' In this BP, you can substitute another fresh fruit such as blueberries, peaches, or strawberries, and also use frozen fruit, in a pinch. This heartwarming dish is wonderful with your morning coffee, too!"

– Portia Little

Fresh Raspberry Bread Pudding

3 eggs
½ cup plus 1½ tsp. sugar
2 cups milk
4 cups cubed day-old French or Italian bread
¾ cup fresh raspberries
1 Tbsp. butter

With electric mixer, beat eggs until foamy.

Beat in ½ cup sugar. Mix in milk. Place bread cubes in buttered or cooking-sprayed 1½-quart soufflé dish or baking pan. Pour egg mixture over bread. Scatter berries over top of bread, pushing down into mixture.

Dot with slivers of butter and sprinkle with the remaining sugar.

Bake in a 400-degree oven for 45-50 minutes, or until a knife inserted in center comes out clean.

Serve warm with whipped cream or topping.

Yield: 4 – 6 servings.

Source: *Bread Pudding Bliss* by Portia Little

David Long

A Massachusetts native, David Long graduated from Albion College. While at the University of Montana's MFA program, Long studied under Richard Hugo, Bill Kittredge and Madeline DeFrees. His early published works include a book of poems and three books of stories. Long's first novel, *The Falling Boy*, was published in 1997 and was followed by *The Daughters of Simon Lamoreaux* and *The Inhabited World*. His fiction has appeared in *The New Yorker*, *GQ*, *Story* and numerous other publications. Long is the recipient of an O. Henry Award, a Pushcart Prize, a Rosenthal Prize from the American Academy of Arts and Letters in addition to many other honors.

After living in Kalispell, Montana, for many years, Long relocated to Tacoma. He is married to Susan Long, a medical librarian, and they have two grown sons, Montana and Jackson.

ABOUT THE RECIPE:

"I'm a huge fan of the Crock-Pot® – slow-cooked pork (and chicken) simply tastes better. By the way, I've had great luck with Costco pork loins – lean, dependable. This recipe comes from my friend and neighbor, Joan Wekell. I think I'll make it again tonight."

– David Long

Chile Verde

1½ lbs. pork tenderloin, cubed
24 oz. jar green salsa
14 oz. jar diced green chilies
1-2 large chopped onions (Walla Walla sweets preferred)
Several cloves of garlic, minced
1 tsp. dried oregano
1 tsp. cumin
2 cans Cannelini beans, un-drained
1 can whole kernel corn

Mix all ingredients and cook in a Crock-Pot® or 250 degree oven for at least four hours. Add a can of whole kernel corn and heat a while longer.

Add a dollop of sour cream when serving.

Accompany with corn bread or corn chips.

Richard Louv

The author of seven books, Richard Louv has most recently written *Last Child in the Woods: Saving Our Children From Nature-Deficit Disorder*. Among his other books are *Childhood's Future*, *The Web of Life*, *Fly-Fishing for Sharks: An Angler's Journey Across America* and *America II*.

He is a columnist for *The San Diego Union-Tribune* and has written for *The New York Times*, *The Washington Post*, and numerous newspapers and magazines. He served as a columnist and on the editorial advisory board for *Parents* magazine. He is an advisor to the Ford Foundation's Leadership for a Changing World award program and the Scientific Council on the Developing Child. He is a Visiting Scholar at the Heller School for Social Policy and Management at Brandeis University. He helped found Connect for Kids, the largest child advocacy Internet site. Louv has appeared frequently as a guest on national radio and television programs. He spoke before the National Policy Council at the White House.

He is married to Kathy Frederick Louv and is the father two sons. Reach him at rlouv@cts.com or via www.thefuturesedge.com.

ABOUT THE RECIPE:

"Our whole family loves this treat and it's low fat, low calorie."

– Richard Louv

My Wife Kathy's Parfaits

12-oz. crushed pineapple in natural juice, undrained
1 3.5-oz. box sugar free instant vanilla pudding
2 cup fat-free or low-fat milk
4 oz. fat-free cream cheese, at room temperature
1 8-oz. carton of fat-free or "lite" Cool Whip® topping, defrosted
½ cup flaked or shredded coconut
½ cup chopped pecans

1. Mix instant pudding and milk, following instructions on box.

2. Mix cream cheese and Cool Whip with electric mixer just until blended.

3. Alternate layers of pudding, pineapple, and Cool Whip mixture in 6 - 8 parfait or wine glasses.

4. Top with coconut, then pecans.

5. Chill one hour before serving.

This dessert can also be layered in a serving bowl or a plastic container for a picnic.

Serves 6 – 8

Margaret Read MacDonald

A former King County, Washington librarian, Margaret Read MacDonald just loves folktales. She reads them, tells them, writes them down…shapes them into picture books…and writes scholarly books about the folks who tell them. *Ten Traditional Tellers* shares interviews with tellers from around the globe, including the Pacific Northwest's own Vi Hilbert, Curtis DuPuis, Rinjing Dorje, and Won-Ldy Paye. As the author of more than 45 books, this popular folklorist travels the globe telling old tales and discovering new ones.

PUBLISHED WORKS:

Five Minute Tales: More Stories to Read and Tell When Time is Short; Peace Tales: World Folktales to Talk About; The Great Smelly, Slobbery, Small-Toothed Dog: A Folktale from Great Britain; Twenty Tellable Tales; Earth Care: World Folktales to Talk About and *Conejito: A Folktale from Panama*.

ABOUT THE RECIPE:

"I spend my time at the typewriter…not in the kitchen…so my daughters missed out on the 'cooking with Mom' lessons. But thanks to Aunt Sally's Creamed Corn recipe, they are still able to hold up their heads just fine when it is their turn to 'bring a dish.'

Aunt Sally Read Johnston was a librarian at the University of Washington Law Library. So she read more than she cooked, too. But she did come across this one sure-fire and really quick recipe. You can whip it up and be back at your computer (or with your nose back in the book where it belongs) in no time flat."

— *Margaret Read McDonald*

Aunt Sally's Creamed Corn

1 can cream corn
1 can corn kernels, strained
8 oz. sour cream or yogurt
1 stick real butter
1 egg
1 box Jiffy® corn muffin mix

Whip egg and softened butter with fork. Pour in all ingredients and mix thoroughly…no lumps. Pour into greased pan. Bake at 375 degrees for an hour or until brown and crispy on top.

Layne Maheu

Author Layne Maheu lives with his son in Seattle, where he works as a carpenter. His short stories have appeared in *Other Voices*, *Northwest Review*, *Ascent* and elsewhere. *Song of the Crow* is his debut novel, which tells the story of Noah's Ark from the perspective of a crow named "I Am."

ABOUT THE RECIPE:

"Hunger is the best sauce. So they say. And in my mind, the following is second, unless you combine it with hunger.

I learned of this sauce when I was a deckhand aboard a commercial fishing vessel in South East Alaska, a 58-foot purse-seiner that went after salmon. Though we caught the fish by the ton, oddly enough, the marinade was put on steaks. I myself, however, have never used the marinade for anything other than fish. Over the years, I've made a few innovations to the recipe, which I'll include.

Even non-fish-eaters love this marinade on salmon. Children say it tastes like candy. Enjoy."

– Layne Maheu

Paulita's Teriyaki Marinade

1. Add equal parts of soy sauce and molasses.

2. Add chopped fresh garlic and fresh ginger.

3. Throw it all together.

So long as you can taste each of these ingredients in the marinade, you cannot go wrong.*

Here are a few innovations on a theme:

- Throw in a generous portion of lime juice (fresh-squeezed is best).
- Chop up some cilantro, too, lots, and throw in that.

So, in short: half-soy sauce, half-molasses, and half-hunger. Then chop up your garlic and ginger, and then throw in some lime juice and cilantro. Then marinade your barbecue beast – chickenbeeflambwhatever – though I recommend fish, especially salmon.

*Note: Because the marinade is salty, it will pickle the fish in its brine and take away its translucency if you marinade it for more then two hours before grilling.

Susan McBride

Award-winning author Susan McBride has penned five Debutante Dropout Mysteries and will debut her first Young Adult series with *The Debs*. Called "The Lou's Whodunit Queen" by *Sauce Magazine* in St. Louis, Susan was selected as one of the city's "Top Singles" in 2005 by *St. Louis Magazine*, but is single no more. She tied the knot in late February of 2008! For more scoop on Susan, visit her web site at SusanMcBride.com.

PUBLISHED WORKS:

The Debutante Dropout Mysteries: *Blue Blood, The Good Girl's Guide to Murder, The Lone Star Lonely Hearts Club, Night of the Living Deb* and *Too Pretty to Die.*

ABOUT THE RECIPE:

"As anyone who knows me understands, I'm no Martha Stewart in the kitchen. Everyone at the Whole Foods deli counter can recognize me by sight, if not by name. And, I keep our local Domino's on speed-dial (love thin crust with green peppers and onions!). So it's rare that I actually whip up anything from scratch. But when I do, I like it to be as healthy as possible. I appreciate quick and easy, too, like my favorite recipe for Spinach-Artichoke Dip. It's low in fat, quick and easy to pair with yummy whole-grain crackers, chips or pita bread. Though, if you're craving carbs and feeling decadent, go ahead and smear it on French bread without feeling too much guilt!"

— *Susan McBride*

Spinach-Artichoke Dip

1 cup light mayonnaise or soy mayo
1 cup grated nonfat or low-fat Parmesan cheese
1 can (14 oz) artichoke hearts, drained and chopped
1 package (10 oz) frozen chopped spinach, thawed and drained
1/2 cup shredded skim mozzarella cheese

1. Heat oven to 350 degrees. Mix mayo and Parmesan cheese. Stir in artichoke hearts and spinach.

2. Spoon mixture into a one-quart casserole dish. Sprinkle with shredded mozzarella until covered.

3. Bake about 20 minutes until cheese is melted. Serve warm with chips, crackers or pita.

Enjoy!

Kaya McLaren

Kaya McLaren's books are quirky, humorous, heart-wrenching, sweet, and perhaps slightly magical as they explore what family can be. *Church of the Dog* and *On the Divinity of Second Chances* are followed by McLaren's new novel, *How I Came to Sparkle Again*, which will be published in 2009.

Kaya has worked as an archaeologist, a massage therapist, and an art teacher. Currently she teaches third and fourth grade at Easton School on Snoqualmie Pass, in Washington. When she's not teaching or writing, she's telemark skiing, cross-country skiing, skate-skiing, swimming in lakes with her dog, singing and playing bass at "open mic night" at the local coffee house, skateboarding, painting, belly dancing and surfing.

ABOUT THE RECIPE:

"When I first moved to Sun Valley, Idaho, I bought a package of cookies from the Simple Kneads Bakery at the store, and they rocked my world. I wrote Mari Wania, the baker, a fan letter and asked if she wanted to trade baked goods for massage (that's how I was making my living). To my delight, Mary said yes. We traded for a couple years and they were the most delicious two years of my life. After I relocated,

I offered to fill in for her at her one-woman business, providing she would teach me how to bake. The following summer, she took me up on it. The base of this cookie recipe I learned from her, but I exchanged some flour for oats, and made up the rest. If you're in Sun Valley, go to Atkinson's or William's (grocery stores) and pick up a couple different bags of Mari's cookies, or better yet, her cinnamon rolls. Mmm!"

– Kaya McLaren

Kaya's Cookies

When I make these cookies, I do measure my butter, sugar, vanilla, salt, baking soda, and flour. After that though, I just start dumping things in.

2 sticks of butter (or use ¹/₂ cup canola shortening or soy margarine
    instead of one stick)
¹/₂ cup pure maple syrup or honey or any combination
¹/₂ cup date sugar or sucrose or organic turbinado sugar
2 Tbsp. molasses (optional)
1 tsp. real vanilla
¹/₄ cup water (you may need more to make the texture right)
2 cups whole-wheat pastry flour
1 cups oats
¹/₃ cup millet (optional, but I love the crunch)
¹/₂ tsp. salt
¹/₂ tsp. baking soda
1 Tbsp. cinnamon
1¹/₂ cups coconut (toast it in the oven to take it to the next level)
¹/₂ cup crushed almonds
2 cups chocolate chips
1 cup Craisins® (optional), dried currents, or dried cherries

Cream the butter and sugars. Stir the salt, baking soda, and cinnamon right into the measuring cup of flour with a knife and blend that with the sugar-butter mix. Dump in oats, millet, and water. You may need to add a little more water to get the texture just right. Now dump in all the goodies – the coconut, almonds, dried fruit if you want, and chocolate chips. If you choose to lightly toast the coconut on a cookie sheet until golden brown, the coconut will be crunchier. And if it's still hot, the chocolate chips will melt, making it a chocolaty cookie. But it doesn't matter, because they always turn out delicious.

The recipe is just a suggestion. It's not rocket science. Enjoy making it your own. I like big, fat cookies. So, I use an ice cream scoop to scoop out the dough. After I plop it on the cookie sheet, I squish it a little because they don't flatten out like other less-fibrous cookies. Bake for about 14 minutes at 325 degrees. Note: They don't brown up like other cookies if you use mostly maple syrup, so don't be fooled.

Alexander McCall Smith

An author of more than 60 books, Alexander McCall Smith has written academic titles, short story collections plus a number of immensely popular children's books. Referred to as the new P.G. Wodehouse, he is best known for his internationally acclaimed *No. 1 Ladies Detective Agency* series, which rapidly rose to the top of the bestseller lists throughout the world.

The Sunday Philosophy Club, 44 Scotland Street and *Portuguese Irregular Verb* series also delight readers around the world. His children's books, including the *Akimbo* series, are about a boy in Africa. His collection of African folktales is featured in *The Girl Who Married a Lion.*

Born in Bulawayo, Rhodesia, McCall Smith was educated at CBC Bulawayo before moving to Scotland to study law at the University of Edinburgh. After returning to southern Africa to teach law at the University of Botswana, he returned once more to Edinburgh, where he lives today with his wife, Elizabeth, an Edinburgh physician, and their two daughters Lucy and Emily. He was a professor of medical law at the University of Edinburgh and is now an emeritus professor at its school of law. He is an amateur bassoonist and co-founder of The Really Terrible Orchestra.

ABOUT THE RECIPE:

"The recipe here represents one of the delicious things in the world. My Mma Potokwani's fruitcake can be a little on the heavy side for some tastes. However, it has the merit of being undoubtedly what it is. If you close your eyes, you are left in no doubt as to what you are eating. Can one say that about nouvelle cuisine?"

– Alexander McCall Smith

Mma Potokwani's Fruit Cake

6 oz. unsalted butter, softened
6 oz. caster (superfine) sugar
Grated zest of 1 orange (or a teaspoon of English Seville marmalade)
4 medium eggs
2 oz. ground almonds
6 oz. all-purpose flour
1 tsp. baking powder
1 tsp. mixed spices (cinnamon, nutmeg, allspice and cloves)
12 oz. dried fruits (this can be a mixture raisins, sultanas, currants, etc.)
2 oz. mixed peel (glace fruit)
1 Tbsp. water

Pre-heat the oven to 330 degrees. Cream the butter, sugar and orange zest (or marmalade) until it is light and fluffy. Then, beat in the eggs, one at a time. Add a little of the flour if the mixture begins to curdle.

Sieve in the sifted flour, baking powder and spices. Then, add the ground almonds and fold everything together. Stir in the dried fruit and mixed peel. Add the water until the mixture has a soft consistency.

Grease and line a 7-inch cake tin. Spoon the mixture into the tin and smooth the top of it. Bake for about 1½ to 2 hours, until cooked through. Test for doneness with a toothpick.

Cool the cake in the tin before turning it out on a cooling rack. Serve to your friends with a cup of Red Bush tea.

Makes one cake

Brad Meltzer

Photo by Herman Estevez

Attorney and screenwriter Brad Meltzer is the author of *The New York Times* bestseller *The Book of Fate* and five other bestselling thrillers: *The Tenth Justice, Dead Even, The First Counsel, The Millionaires* and *The Zero Game*. He is also one of the co-creators of the TV show, Jack & Bobby, and is the writer of the top-selling graphic novels *Identity Crisis* and *Justice League of America.* His newest comic book is *DC Universe*, and his new thriller, *The Book of Lies,* is now available.

Brad currently lives in Florida with his wife, who is also an attorney. They both love this chicken recipe.

ABOUT THE RECIPE:

"It wasn't until I graduated from college that I got involved in writing. I was coming out of the University of Michigan and I had a job offer from the man who used to run *Games* magazine. He told me, 'If you love the job, you'll stay. If you hate it, you'll leave a year later with some money in your pocket.' Since I had some debt to pay off, that seemed like a fair deal. So I moved all my stuff to Boston. But when I got there, the publisher left the magazine. (Surprise!) The whole reason I went there was to work for him. I thought I'd wrecked my life. I had no idea what to do.

So I did what all of us would do in that situation. I said, 'I'm gonna write a novel.' And I just started writing. Every day, I just fell more and more in love with the process."

– Brad Meltzer

Italian Chicken

1 cut-up chicken
1 cup Italian salad dressing
1 can mushrooms, stems and pieces, drained
Parmesan cheese, grated
Seasoned salt
Pepper
Garlic salt

Pre-heat oven to 350 degrees. Prepare Pam® non-stick spray on a baking dish.

1. Clean and season the chicken to taste. Brush Italian dressing on the skin side of the chicken pieces and place, skin side down, in the baking dish.

2. Brush remaining dressing on the chicken. If you do not have enough dressing for each piece, just add more until each piece is coated.

3. Bake the chicken for 30 minutes. Remove from the oven and turn each piece of chicken so the skin side is up.

4. Put mushrooms around the chicken. Sprinkle cheese on top of the chicken and return it to the oven for 30 – 40 minutes or until it is nicely browned.

Jacquelyn Mitchard

Novelist and screenplay writer, Jacquelyn Mitchard, is the author of *The New York Times* bestselling novel, *The Deep End of the Ocean*, which was chosen as the first book for Oprah Winfrey's Book Club and named by *USA Today* as one of the most influential books of the past 25 years. She has subsequently written seven bestselling novels, *The Most Wanted, A Theory of Relativity, Twelve Times Blessed, Christmas, Present, The Breakdown Lane, Cage of Stars* and *Still Summer* plus an essay collection, *The Rest of Us: Dispatches From the Mothership*. The film version of *The Deep End of the Ocean*, was released in 1999. *Still Summer*, is now in development for a "Lifetime" original film and *Cage of Stars* is set for a film treatment.

Mitchard has published four books for children, *Starring Prima!; Rosalie, My Rosalie; Baby Bat's Lullaby* and *Ready, Set, School!* Her first novel for young adults, *Now You See Her*, was followed by *All We Know of Heaven* and *The Midnight Twins*.

A former syndicated columnist, Mitchard is now is a contributing editor for *Wondertime* magazine and a frequent contributor to magazines including *Parade, Reader's Digest, Ladies' Home Journal, More* and *Real Simple*. Her screenplays include A Serpent's Egg and Doing Fine.

A Ragdale Foundation Distinguished Fellow, she has also written two non-fiction books, *Mother Less Child: The Love Story of a Family* and *Jane Addams of Hull House*. She is the founding organizer of One Writer's Place, a small residence for writers and artists healing through creativity after difficult life circumstances. Mitchard lives in Wisconsin with her husband Christopher Brent, and their seven children. Her website is: www.jackiemitchard.com.

ABOUT THE RECIPE:

"I make a double recipe of TuTu, and I set aside a whole day for construction and cleanup. They don't just dirty up the kitchen, they lay waste to the kitchen. Cookies that require more than a dozen ingredients are a waste of time unless you make enough for an army. And, don't think that 18 dozen is enough for an army. These will disappear in moments unless you sneak large foil-covered trays to the garage and freeze them. I start freezing them in October. The first thing my five-year-old learned to say was 'TuTu.' And, the first thing our college kids ask for at Christmas break is a big cold glass of milk and TuTus. No Italian family worth its red sauce would celebrate without them, and just thinking of them reminds me of dark skies threatening snow and a 15-foot tree. *Buon Appetito!*"

– Jacquelyn Mitchard

TuTus

$5^{1}/_{2}$ cups flour
1 tsp. baking soda
1 Tbsp. baking powder
$^{1}/_{4}$ tsp. salt
$^{1}/_{2}$ cup cocoa powder (unsweetened)
$^{3}/_{4}$ cup granulated sugar
$^{1}/_{2}$ cup brown sugar
$^{1}/_{2}$ cup (1 stick) butter
$^{1}/_{2}$ cup vegetable shortening
1 cup coarsely chopped walnuts
3 eggs, slightly beaten
1 Tbsp. vanilla extract
$^{1}/_{2}$ cup brewed coffee at room temperature

In large mixing bowl, combine flour, baking soda, baking powder, salt, cocoa, granulated and brown sugars. Mix well. With hands or pastry blender, cut butter and vegetable shortening into a dry mixture, as for piecrust, until the consistency is of coarse cornmeal. Stir in nuts.

In another bowl, combine eggs, vanilla and coffee. Add to flour mixture. Mix well. Form balls of dough about ³/₄ inch in diameter. Place on un-greased cookie sheet.

Bake at 350 degrees for 10-12 minutes until lightly browned.

Prepare frosting (see recipe below). Take a few cookies at a time and dip into frosting, turning with your hand until cookies are completely covered. Shake off excess frosting over bowl. Place cookies on wire rack to dry 3-6 hours.

Sprinkle colored sugar or sprinkles on immediately after placing on racks.

Frosting
¹/₂ cup milk
1¹/₂ pounds powdered sugar (about 6 cups)
1 tsp. vanilla

In bowl, stir milk into powdered sugar. Add vanilla. Mix until smooth. Stir in more milk if needed to obtain a thin consistency (a little thicker than maple syrup).

Linda A. Mohr

Educator, columnist, entrepreneur, and eternal animal lover, Linda Mohr teaches marketing and management at Northwood University in Florida. She is the author of *Tatianna—Tales and Teachings of My Feline Friend* and *Catnip Connection*. Her blog appears in *The Seattle Post-Intelligencer* newspaper and at her web site www.lindamohr.net. She pioneered the first one-stop Pet Apothecary in Palm Beach County. Her education includes a BS degree from University of Missouri, a MS from Purdue University, and an MBA from Nova Southeastern.

ABOUT THE RECIPE:

"The Apple Crisp recipe is a scrumptious selection for today's busy woman who still desires to serve dessert. The recipe was passed down to me from my mother. We prepare this old-fashioned, comforting dessert often. It requires common ingredients and is quick and easy to assemble from scratch. Sometimes, I substitute peaches. Always a hit with my family and friends!"

– Linda Mohr

Apple Crisp

5 cups sliced apples (for baking)
1 cup flour
1 cup brown sugar
¾ cup quick oatmeal
1 tsp. cinnamon
½ tsp. salt
½ cup butter

Place apples in an 8" x 12" pan.

Combine rest of ingredients and cut in butter. Sprinkle topping over the apples.

Bake on "High" setting uncovered for 15 minutes in microwave oven or until the apples are tender. Rotate the dish half way through the baking process.

Serve with whipped cream or vanilla ice cream, if desired.

Serves 6

Skye Moody

A professional writer all of her adult life, Skye Moody writes both fiction and nonfiction, and has had published more than 80 essays, short stories, one-act plays, and poems. Her books have won a Mademoiselle Woman of the Year Award and a President's Award from the National Endowment for the Humanities. Before turning full-time to fiction writing, she worked for 25 years as an international journalist and photojournalist, winning critical acclaim for her first two books of nonfiction, *Hillbilly Women* and *Fruits of Our Labor: Soviet & American Workers Talk About Making a Living.*

Covering social and environmental issues, Moody has traveled throughout the world, primarily in Third World and developing nations, including China, Uzbekistan, Armenia, Tajikistan, Georgia, and Russia, including northeastern Siberia, and East Africa. On location, she has covered such subjects as Chinese and Russian coal mining, reindeer herding in northern Siberia, textile mills and farming in Uzbekistan, river pollution in the Republic of Georgia, and the effects of acid rain in the Arctic Circle.

Seven novels in her endangered species mystery series include: *Rain Dance, Blue Poppy, Wildcrafters, Habitat, K Falls, Medusa* and *The Good Diamond.*

ABOUT THE RECIPE:

"I can't cook. I have flooded kitchens, set them afire, caused microwave meltdowns, roasted guinea hens with the giblet packets still inside, burned myself, burned others, prepared revolting gravies and baked *éclairs* that looked and tasted like fried eggs. I am generally banned from kitchens. And so, for this contribution to *Literary Feast*, I turn to my dear friend, the actor Douglas Barden, of New Orleans.

This six-ingredient dessert is among the most romantic, sensual delicacies enjoyed in New Orleans. Easy to prepare, this dessert can be transformed into a tableside drama by measuring out all the ingredients beforehand and preparing the sauce at table on that little French flambeau cart-on-wheels we all have stashed in our pantries…or over a Sterno flame…or outdoors over a campfire. As the French say *C'est le petit Jésus en culottes de velours*! (It is like God in velvet culottes.)"

— *Skye Moody*

Barden's New Orleans Banana Foster

2 Tbsp. butter
2 Tbsp. brown sugar
1 banana, sliced
1 oz. Bols' Crème de Banana Liqueur
1 oz. white rum
Dash of cinnamon

You'll need: A gas flame or 1 long match. (No BICs allowed!)
Optional: Two scoops of vanilla ice cream

In an open sauté pan over medium high heat, add the butter and sugar until they become bubbly. Then, add the banana and cinnamon. Once the mixture is heated through, remove the pan from the heat and add the liqueur and rum. Carefully, swirl the mixture with one hand as you light the sauce with the match in the other. Stand back until the flames subside. Serve immediately on two warm plates.

Serves 2

John J. Nance

No writer has taken readers into the high drama and sheer terror of modern air travel more successfully than pilot and aviation analyst John J. Nance. With bestsellers *Final Approach, Scorpion, Strike, Phoenix Rising, Pandora's Clock, The Last Hostage, Headwind, Skyhook* and *Fire Flight*, this master of the aviation thriller has carved a territory all his own.

The popular author is a native Texan who grew up in Dallas and holds a bachelor's degree from SMU plus a juris doctorate from SMU School of Law. He is a licensed attorney and former airline pilot. In addition, John is a seasoned broadcaster and air-safety consultant for ABC television. He lives in University Place, Washington, and maintains a website at www.john-nance.com.

ABOUT THE RECIPE:

"Coming from Texas, Chili is somewhere between a responsibility and an offshoot religion (read: cult). No self-respecting Texas male fails to barbeque, and no self-respecting Texan worthy of his or her passport from Austin (that's our capitol, okay?) fails to carry the "Chili Gene" around on a 24-7 basis. That simply means, given the opportunity, we know how to toss enough fixins into a pot to make a passable Chili. (And yes, by Texas law, Chili is ALWAYS capitalized.)

This recipe was my response to the great Chili cook-off in Terlingua, Texas, held annually amidst rattlesnakes and rivers of beer. And, yes, if you must, you can 'Californize' it with sour cream and other unspeakable ingredients, but please try it without the beans. If God had meant Chili to have beans, Texas would still belong to Mexico. Oh, wait a minute, half of it does!"

– John Nance

After-Burner Chili

1½ pounds of high-quality steak, cooked medium and then cut into ½ inch pieces
OR
1½ pounds of all-natural ground beef, cooked and drained
    thoroughly

Beef choice from above and cook over low flame
Mix in 2 small cans of tomato paste
1 cup water
Mix in 2 Tbsp. cumin
4 Tbsp. chili powder
¾ cup chopped onion (Walla Walla sweets preferred)
1 Tbsp. cinnamon
⅛ cup of sugar

Note: If you want beans (real chili doesn't have beans), simmer one cup of pintos for three hours on the side in water.

Add corn starch if necessary to thicken
Add black pepper, cumin and onions to taste
And ⅛ cup chopped jalapenos
Stir and simmer for four hours.
Add the beans (if you must) and serve

Serves 2 teenagers or a family of 6

Katherine Neville

Photo by Kelley Campbell Photography

World traveler Katherine Neville is the bestselling author of international thrillers *The Eight*, *A Calculated Risk*, and *The Magic Circle*. Her books are in print in more than 30 languages, and have received numerous awards. Katherine's prior career as an international computer wizard took her to live in six countries on three continents and in more than half of the states in the U.S., where she draws from her experiences to write colorful novels. Par for the course, her next thriller, *The Fire*, the sequel to the popular *The Eight*, takes place in Russia, Colorado, Albania, Rome, Morocco, Alaska, and her own backyard of Washington, DC.

ABOUT THE RECIPE:

"I enjoy creating a rich international flavor with my books' characters. This hearty, slow-cooking recipe is from my newest novel that is a globe-trotting feast. As Alexandra Solarin would do, just serve it with steamed new potatoes and a fresh green salad. *Bon Appetit!*"

– *Katherine Neville*

Alexandra Solarin's Open-Hearth Boeuf Bourguignon

3 lbs. beef cut in cubes
6 chopped shallots
2 celery stalks, sliced, including leaves
3 garlic cloves, minced
1 lb. packaged baby carrots
1 lb. sliced mushrooms
½ bunch parsley, chopped finely
3 crumbled bay leaves
1 Tbsp. thyme
1 Tbsp. Italian herbs or *Hérbes de Provence*
Vegetable oil
Cognac
Worcestershire sauce
Lemon juice
Dry red wine
Homemade beef stock or canned beef broth
Salt and pepper

In a large skillet with just enough vegetable oil to coat the bottom, sauté beef in batches of 15-20 cubes, turning quickly to seal all sides. Remove cubes to a large casserole dish with a cover.

In the same pan, reduce heat to medium. Sauté the shallots, celery, garlic, and baby carrots until shallots are golden, scraping up any stuck meat (about 10 minutes). Pour this concoction over the beef cubes in a large casserole dish.

To the casserole, add the raw mushrooms, chopped parsley, all the herbs, salt and pepper, a splash each of Cognac, Worcestershire, and lemon juice. Toss well so everything is mixed.

Add wine and beef stock, in equal amounts, until ingredients are barely covered (about 3 cups each). If using canned beef stock, which is very salty, mix in ½ cup of water for each cup of stock.

Cover casserole and bake in a preheated 350 degree oven for 2 hours or until cubes are tender. If liquid boils too low, add more.

Serves 6 – 8

From *The Fire*, October 2008

Kevin O'Brien

Before his thrillers landed him on *The New York Times* bestseller list, Kevin O'Brien made his living as a railroad inspector and did all his writing at night. His second novel, *Only Son*, was optioned for film rights, thanks to interest from Tom Hanks, and also was chosen by *Readers Digest* for its Select Editions. His third novel – and first thriller, *The Next to Die* – jumped up the bestseller charts. He's been writing full-time ever since.

O'Brien's last three thrillers have all been *New York Times* bestsellers, most recently, *One Last Scream*. Kevin lives in Seattle, loves Hitchcock movies, and his tenth novel, *Final Breath*, was released in December 2008.

ABOUT THE RECIPE:

"I was born in 1955, the same year Campbell's Soup developed the recipe for that famous 'Green Bean Casserole' someone always brings to potlucks and Thanksgiving dinners. This should give you an idea of my dietary staples growing up. I lived in Chicago's North Shore, the youngest of six kids. My mom knew how to stretch a meal and make comfort food from leftovers. When I moved to Seattle in 1980, I asked my mother for the recipes for some of my favorite dinners. Nearly all of them called for Campbell's 'Cream of Something Soup' and cheese. In fact, I still have the piece of paper on which I scribbled the recipes while my mother dictated. Now yellowed, food-stained, and falling apart, it looks like some document from the Civil War. My mom died in 1992, but I still enjoy the dinner recipes she passed on to me.

The following dish is real comfort food. My mother used to call it 'Nothing-Noodle Casserole.' I'm not sure why – maybe because very little preparation or cooking time is required. I just remember when I was a kid, on those nights when I'd ask mom what was for dinner, and she'd answer, 'Nothing.' Then she'd wait a beat, 'Noodle Casserole!' It always made me smile."

– Kevin O'Brien

Adele O'Brien's Nothing-Noodle Casserole

Medium/large egg noodles (approximately 3-4 cups)
Leftover pot roast and gravy
1 can Campbell's Cream of Mushroom soup
½ cup sour cream
Grated Parmesan cheese

Preheat the oven to 350 degrees.

Boil noodles in salted water and drain. While the noodles are boiling, cut the pot roast into small, bite-sized pieces. Grease a large casserole bowl. Dump the noodles, pot roast, gravy, mushroom soup and sour cream into the bowl. Sprinkle liberally with Parmesan cheese. Cover with foil, and pop it in the oven.

Bake for 25-30 minutes. Peel off the foil and let bake uncovered for another 5 minutes – until the top is lightly browned and crusty. Serve with asparagus or broccoli. Make plans to add 15 minutes to your workout the next day!

Substitutions: Use spaghetti in place of egg noodles (break in half before boiling). Use freshly cooked ground beef instead of pot roast. Try low-sodium, low-fat soup, and low-fat sour cream.

The chicken alternative: Sauté 4 chicken breasts, cut up and let stand in butter, a bit of chicken broth, and a little white wine. Use cream of chicken instead of cream of mushroom soup.

Serves 4 – 6

Sam Okamoto

Internationally acclaimed master chef Osamu "Sam" Okamoto has rolled onto the culinary landscape with traditional cooking techniques and new ways to look at food.

Okamoto originally trained as a French chef in his native Japan at the Hakata Imperial Hotel in Kita-Kyushi City. He later studied under master chef Marcel Kretz at La Sapineire in Quebec, Canada, listed by *TIME* magazine as one of the top three hotel restaurants in the country. Returning to his Asian roots while searching for an alternative to the typical North American diet, Chef Okamoto moved to Vancouver, British Columbia, where he worked extensively with restaurant owners, revamping their menus to incorporate healthy recipes and cooking styles. He provided culinary style at Briar Avenue and Hatopoppo restaurants on Vancouver's trendy Robson Street.

Chef Okamoto is the author of *Sam Okamoto's Incredible Vegetables* and developed food for Hollywood films including *Alive!, Shoot to Kill* and *The Adventures of Yellow Dog*. Okamoto also served as the personal chef for Academy Award-winner Sidney Poitier and his family.

ABOUT THE RECIPE:

"Your body is a well-oiled machine that requires constant maintenance and care. Just like your car, it must have ether right fuels and if not fed properly, it will not run as efficiently or as long. And picking the right foods to fuel yourself is not as easy as checking an octane rating. This recipe will give you the right fuel to go. An adaptation of a famous French soup, using a combination of caramelized onion, garlic, and miso to create a rich 'East meets West' flavor you'll enjoy. The key to success is not to burn the onions while cooking. Brown them with caution and care."

– Sam Okamoto

Onion Miso Soup

4 - 5 Tbsp. oil
6 large onions, thinly sliced
2 Tbsp. minced garlic
1 leek (white part only) well washed and thinly sliced
8 cups water
Pinch whole thyme
2 bay leaves
4 - 5 Tbsp. red miso
Salt and pepper to taste

Heat a large, heavy pot and add oil and sauté onion garlic and leek until onions are almost caramelized, about 2 hours.

Add water, thyme, and bay leaves. Then simmer for one hour, skimming from time to time.

Add miso, stir, and cook for another two the three minutes.

Season to taste with salt and pepper.

Remove bay leaves and serve in individual soup bowls.

Serves 8

Julie Oliver

An award-winning artist, poet, and essayist, Julie Johnson Oliver is an eclectic author of magazine articles, a health newsletter, ad copy/design, website text, brochures, children's stories, and assorted scripts. As a playwright, her 1964 *I Love Lucy* parody performed with cousins in grandma's basement received unrivaled reviews. People still talk about it 40 years later. Her scripts include three well-received musicals, two feature-length screenplays and one short film.

Ms. Oliver's most cherished award was first place in the 1965 Blackfoot, Idaho city-wide poetry competition for "Geese Flying in a V." She can still recite most of it…and does so when her husband of more than 31 years needs a *soupçon* of culture. (Not that we can pronounce that word.) She loves him and their four children, their spouses, and grandchildren a ton. (Which is way more than a *soupçon.*)

Ms. Oliver holds a B.S. in Law Enforcement and Justice Administration; is a member of artist/writer organizations; holds ongoing teacher/leadership positions in her church; and is a community volunteer. Her talents have allowed her an wide range of business experiences. Her life adventures, both joyful and traumatic, have served her well, leading to this very moment: her debut book, *I've Been 16 for 34 Years – a BoomerTweener™ memoir*. More are on the way, once she recovers from this one.

She says: "I'm not *famous*. But, my grandbabies and I get along *famously* – a gigantic reward. Brightening the corners of my world with plays, poetry, and performances... I used to want to be famous; but now I'd rather play with family, then curl up with a good book, then eat. I cook, and used to want to cook, but now I'd rather devour treats that close kin, distant relatives, or any skilled stranger in a clean kitchen create. Yes, family, Frost, and fajitas…yum. Contentment counts, and substance trumps fame."

ABOUT THE RECIPE:

"After eating my waffles, you'll agree that Mr. Webster's dictionary needs a new definition for 'waffle.' There is nothing 'vague or indecisive' about this breakfast goody. They make my family groan with delight and panic. That's why we eat these at holiday times or before we hike up Mt. Rainier or swim the San Juan Channel. Even big eaters find it hard to handle such a robust, satisfying, filling and healthy batter cake. *I've Been 16 for 34 Years*™ and if you have, too, you may still have some 'waffle-stompers' in your closet. Great shoes with action traction on the soles, guaranteed to find you fun times and high adventure? Yes, named after my waffles. International Strong Man competitors? Can only lift four of my waffles at one time. Titanic – sunk by iceberg? No – sunk by a Hearty Hardy Waffle. Disappearing dinosaurs? Tried to eat six in one sitting. Jimmy Hoffa – accessorized in ball and chain? No, it was waffle and chain. Okay, you may have found that last piece of trivia in poor taste, but you'll find my waffles scrumptious, warm, friendly, vigorous and nourishing. Eat at your own risk."

– Julie Oliver

Julie O's Hearty Hardy Waffles

1 cup cornmeal
1 cup sifted flour
2 tsp. baking powder
1 tsp. salt
1 Tbsp. honey
2 eggs
1½ cup milk
½ cup olive oil
½ cup soy milk
1 cup Julie's homemade granola… (or any sugar-free granola that contains oats, flax seed, wheat germ, sunflower seeds, coconut, dried fruits, etc.)

In a large mixing bowl, combine the first four ingredients and mix well. Add the honey, eggs, milk, olive oil, and soy milk. Mix well before adding Julie's homemade granola. Bake in a hot waffle iron until browned and crispy or to your desired doneness. Serve with real butter and real maple syrup. Yummy and hearty!

Makes 8-10 squares. Plenty for four people. Pop the leftover waffles in a toaster the next day.

Julie Paschkis

Born in 1957, Julie Paschkis grew up in Pennsylvania, near Philadelphia. Her parents encouraged her to read, to draw, and to make things throughout her childhood.

She attended Germantown Friends School, *Ringerike Folkehogskole* in Norway, Cornell University and the School for American Craftsmen at RIT, where Paschkis received her BFA.

She taught art to grade school children for about eight years. During that time, Paschkis continued to work on her own art and illustration. In 1991, she stopped teaching to commit herself to creating art full time. That art includes painting, illustration, and illustrating a long list of colorful and creative children's books. All of her works are connected in that they are all storytelling.

PUBLISHED WORKS:

Twist: Yoga Poems (with Janet S. Wong, poems); *The Great Smelly, Slobbery, Small-Tooth Dog* (retold by Margaret Read McDonald); *Yellow Elephant: A Bright Bestiary* (with Julie Larios, poems); *Albert the Fix-It Man* (story by Janet Lord) and *Glass Slipper, Gold Sandal* (with author Paul Fleischman), a *New York Times* Notable Book. For more titles, visit www.julie paschkis.com.

ABOUT THE RECIPE:

"My children's books are most clearly storytelling. I see the book as a 32-page painting in service to the story and characters of the book. The commercial and editorial illustration lead me into worlds that I didn't know about before.

I also like to wander without a destination and painting lets me do that. The paintings are open-ended stories, much like the Apple Pudding Cake recipe from my great grandmother shown here."

– Julie Paschkis

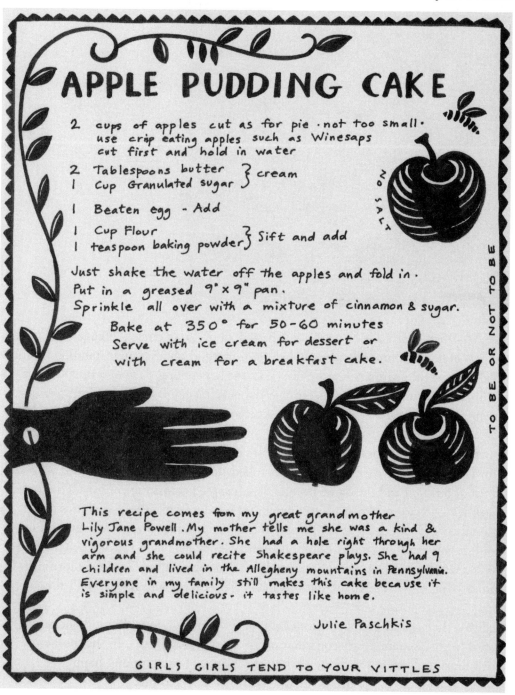

APPLE PUDDING CAKE

2 cups of apples cut as for pie ·not too small· use crisp eating apples such as Winesaps cut first and hold in water

2 Tablespoons butter } cream
1 Cup Granulated sugar

NO SALT

1 Beaten egg - Add

1 Cup Flour
1 teaspoon baking powder } Sift and add

Just shake the water off the apples and fold in.
Put in a greased 9" x 9" pan.
Sprinkle all over with a mixture of cinnamon & sugar.
   Bake at 350° for 50-60 minutes
   Serve with ice cream for dessert or
   with cream for a breakfast cake.

TO BE OR NOT TO BE

This recipe comes from my great grandmother Lily Jane Powell. My mother tells me she was a kind & vigorous grandmother. She had a hole right through her arm and she could recite Shakespeare plays. She had 9 children and lived in the Allegheny mountains in Pennsylvania. Everyone in my family still makes this cake because it is simple and delicious· it tastes like home.

Julie Paschkis

GIRLS GIRLS TEND TO YOUR VITTLES

Nancy Pearl

Photo by Marco Prozzo

The New York Times calls Nancy Pearl "the talk of librarian circles." Readers can't get enough of her recommendations while bookstores and libraries offer standing room only whenever she visits. Since the release of the best-selling *Book Lust* in 2003 and the librarian action figure modeled in her likeness, Nancy Pearl has become a rock star among readers and the tastemaker people turn to when deciding what to read next.

Having worked as a librarian and bookseller in Detroit, Tulsa, and Seattle, Pearl's knowledge of and love for books is unmatched. In 1998, she developed the program "If All of Seattle Read the Same Book," which spread across the country. The former Executive Director of the Washington Center for the Book, Pearl celebrates the written word by speaking at bookstores and libraries across the country and on her monthly television program "Book Lust with Nancy Pearl" on the Seattle Channel. She is a regular commentator about books on National Public Radio's "Morning Edition" and on NPR affiliate stations KUOW in Seattle and KWGS in Tulsa.

In 2004, she became the 50th winner of the Women's National Book Association Award for her extraordinary contribution to the world of books. In the moments when Pearl finds herself without a book, she is an avid bicyclist and happy grandmother of two. She lives in Seattle with her husband Joe.

PUBLISHED WORKS:

Book Lust: Recommended Reading for Every Mood; Moment and Reason; Book Lust Journal; More Book Lust; Now Read This: A Guide to Mainstream Fiction, 1978-1998; Now Read This II: A Guide to Mainstream Fiction, 1990-2001 and *Book Crush: For Kids and Teens – Recommended Reading for Every Mood, Moment and Interest.*

Drop Scones

2 cups of flour
2 Tbsp. baking powder
1/4 cup sugar
Pinch of salt
1/2 cup butter
2 eggs
1/4 cup cream

Preheat oven to 400 degrees.

Mix flour, baking powder sugar, salt, and butter together until dough resembles coarse meal.

In a separate bowl, combine eggs and cream and beat well.

Pour egg/cream mixture into flour mixture and blend until dry ingredients are just moistened. Do not overmix.

Drop by spoon into mounds on greased baking sheet. Bake until tops are golden, about 15 to 20 minutes. Makes about 10 scones.

I always double the recipe because the scones freeze well. If you want, you can add raisins, currants, dried cranberries, nuts, etc. If so, just add and mix with the dry ingredients before you add the liquids.

Jane Porter

Jane Porter's award-winning 2006 novel, *Flirting with Forty,* was picked by *Redbook Magazine* as its Red Hot Summer Read. It went back for an astounding seven printings in six weeks and was then optioned by Sony Pictures for a Lifetime TV movie. The author of more than 20 bestselling Harlequin titles, Jane won the Golden Heart in 1998, and was a three-time finalist for the prestigious RITA award from Romance Writers of America. Jane currently resides in Bellevue, Washington with her two sons and is looking forward to the release of her next title, *Mrs. Perfect.*

ABOUT THE RECIPE:

"While we're all waiting for *Mrs. Perfect,* consider this Baked Ham Strata. It's delicious for breakfast, brunch or a light supper. Dressed for the occasion, it could serve guests with a Bibb lettuce salad and steamed asparagus."

– Jane Porter

Baked Ham Strata

12 slices firm white bread (i.e., sourdough or French bread)
3 Tbsp. butter, softened
2$\frac{1}{2}$ cups milk
6 large eggs
4 tsp. Dijon-style mustard
$\frac{1}{4}$ tsp. salt
$\frac{1}{4}$ tsp. pepper
$\frac{3}{4}$ - 1 lb. Swiss or Jarlsberg cheese, shredded (I do a mix of cheeses)
$\frac{1}{2}$ - $\frac{3}{4}$ lbs. diced ham
3 green onions chopped (optional)

Toast the bread. Spread one side with butter and cut toast into $\frac{3}{4}$-inch pieces.

In a bowl, whisk together the milk, eggs, mustard, salt and pepper. Butter a 13 x 9-inch baking dish and place half the toast pieces in the dish. Sprinkle toasts with half the cheese, ham and sliced onions. Repeat layering with other half of ingredients.

Slowly pour the egg mixture over the casserole to moisten the toasts. Cover the dish with foil. Refrigerate at least 2 hours or overnight.

Preheat over to 350 degrees. Bake the strata for 45 min. Remove foil and bake 5-10 minutes or until top is lightly browned. Remove from oven and let stand 5 minutes before serving.

Serves 4

Julia Quinn

Quickly earning a reputation for warmth and humor, Julia Quinn's sparkling dialogue is considered among the best in the romance industry. With the release of the much-anticipated *Romancing Mister Bridgerton*, Quinn's novel was voted one of the Top-Ten books of the year by the membership of Romance Writers of America and was a finalist for the RITA Awards in the category of long historical novel. *To Sir Phillip, With Love* received a rare, starred review in the trade magazine *Publishers Weekly*, and was later named by that publication as one of the six best mass-market original novels of the year.

The popularity of the Bridgerton series continued to rise with *When He Was Wicked* and the following *It's in His Kiss*. Both books debuted near the top of *The New York Times* bestseller list.

Quinn released the eighth and final installment in the Bridgerton series of novels: the much-awaited *On the Way to the Wedding*. She currently lives with her family in the Pacific Northwest.

ABOUT THE RECIPE:

"I am strangely unaffected by caffeine, but I still need my morning coffee. It's a ritual for me, whether I am at home, at a coffee bar, or on the road. I thought myself a coffee snob, but while traveling in southern India, I developed a lasting fondness for Nescafé® Instant Coffee. And so, the next time I found myself out of the country for an extended stay, I thought to myself – 'Why bother messing up a coffee maker?'"

– Julia Quinn

Julia Quinn's On-the-Road Instant Coffee

You will need:
Nescafé Instant Coffee
Water
Milk
Sugar
Mug
Spoon

Fill mug with $2/3$ water, $1/3$ milk. Heat in microwave to almost boiling.

Remove carefully. (You never know when those mug handles will get too hot.) Add appropriate amount of Nescafé and sugar. (I don't know how big your mug is, and what's more, I don't know if you even like sugar in your coffee.)

Stir. Drink. Feel free to reheat throughout the day.

Diana Raab

Essayist, memoirist and poet, Diana Raab teaches at the UCLA Writers Program and the Santa Barbara Writers Conference. She is a columnist for InkByte.com, an online magazine for writers. She frequently writes and lectures on journaling.

Raab has released four books and her writing has also appeared in numerous national publications and anthologies. She's the recipient of the Benjamin Franklin Book Award for best health and wellness book for *Getting Pregnant and Staying Pregnant: Overcoming Infertility and High Risk Pregnancy*. It has been translated into French and Spanish. In 2009 the book will be released in its 20th anniversary edition. Visit her website at www.dianaraab.com.

ABOUT THE RECIPE:

"I have an Austrian mother and had a Polish grandmother, so this crispy *Schnitzel* recipe, with home-fried potatoes, was a staple in our home. It was the dish we had once a week and was always served when visitors were invited for dinner. You can say that I was brought up on this meal. Also, it was often accompanied by a sliced cucumber salad marinated in vinegar and water.

Although I didn't mention this recipe in my recently published memoir, *Regina's Closet: Finding My Grandmother's Secret Journal*, it was a huge part of my childhood. My children, now all grown, have also learned to love this favorite dish of their ancestors."

– Diana Raab

Wiener Schnitzel

4 thin slices of "veal scaloppini"
Bowl of flour
Bowl of bread crumbs
2 eggs
Oil
Salt and pepper

Assemble 3 deep bowls: one for the flour; in the second, beat the two eggs; and in the third, put the breadcrumbs. Start with moderate amounts of flour and breadcrumbs, as you can always add more as needed.

Flatten the veal with a meat mallet. Season both sides with salt and pepper. Dip both sides of the veal in the flour. Shake off excess. Dip the flour-coated veal into the egg, making sure veal is completely covered. Lift up and allow excess to drip off. Lay the veal in the breadcrumbs and make sure it gets coated on both sides. To help the breading adhere to the meat during cooking, you can place the cutlets on wax paper in the refrigerator for one hour.

Use a large frying pan and heat oil (can use half oil and half butter) until it gets hot enough that the cutlet sizzles when you put it in. It usually only needs about 2-3 minutes per side. Drain on paper towels. Serve immediately.

This is also delicious served cold for the next day's lunch.

Serves 4

Gloria K. Rand

Working in collaboration with her husband, acclaimed illustrator Ted Rand, Gloria Rand has authored a variety of picture books, from adventure stories based on real-life occurrences to thoughtful works of fiction. She lives on the north shore of Mercer Island, Washington.

PUBLISHED WORKS:

Salty Dog, Salty Sails North, Salty Takes Off, Prince William, A Pen Pal for Max, Mary Was a Little Lamb, Sailing Home, Fighting for the Forest, A Home for Spooky and *Aloha Salty!*

ABOUT THE RECIPE:

"Here's my favorite worry-free dinner. Jambalaya is traditionally made in one pot, with meats and vegetables, and is completed by adding chicken stock. There are two methods of making jambalaya. The first and most common is Creole jambalaya. First, meat is added, usually ham and rice. Then, vegetables and tomatoes are added to cook, then seafood. I've served it to my artist husband, family, friends and guests. Not to be immodest, but they all loved it."

– Gloria Rand

Reb's Famous Jambalaya

1 medium-sized onion, finely chopped
1 green bell pepper, finely chopped
1 8-oz. can "stem and pieces" mushrooms
3 Tbsp. butter

Sauté above ingredients, in a medium-sized covered pot, until tender
and golden brown.

Add:
1 (about 1 lb.) can of diced tomatoes
¼ lb. chopped ham
½ can of okra
1 cup uncooked white rice
1 cup chopped parsley
1 tsp. salt
½ tsp. black pepper
2 bay leaves
½ tsp. ground cloves
½ tsp. chili powder (Spice Island, dark)
¼ tsp thyme
10 drops Tabasco
3 cups water
3 chicken broth cubes (dissolved in the 3 cups of water)
1 lb. large prawns

Mix well, then simmer the above ingredients (except prawns) for about 20 minutes,
covered. Add the prawns, pealed and halved lengthwise. Cook for about 10
minutes more.

Serve with French bread and a salad of thinly sliced oranges, topped with a mixture
of chopped avocado and thin slices of celery. Drizzle with a dressing of olive oil, salt,
and lemon juice.

John Saul

In the thriller genre, John Saul has published 34 *New York Times* bestselling novels. His books have been published worldwide to an adoring public. His six-part serial, *The Blackstone Chronicles*, also appeared on *The New York Times* bestseller list and its CD-ROM game was nominated for Adventure Game of the Year in both 1998 and 1999. An earlier novel, *Cry for the Strangers*, was produced by Gerber Productions and MGM as a CBS Television movie.

ABOUT THE RECIPE:

"This recipe is very simple to prepare. Living in the Pacific Northwest, I used to trap my own Dungeness crabs on Puget Sound. But now, I merely buy it at the store or the Pike Place Market in Downtown Seattle."

— John Saul

Crabby Wabby Casserole

3-4 cups cooked, white rice
1 cup cooked green peas
2 cups cooked Dungeness crab meat
½ chopped onion
4 green onions, chopped
Approximately 3 Tbsp. pimentos
¼ pound butter
½ cup grated Parmesan cheese

Preheat oven to 400 degrees.

Mix the rice, peas, onion, green onion, crab, and pimentos in large casserole dish. Cover the top with Parmesan cheese and dot with butter.

Bake for 15-30 minutes in the oven until the top is slightly brown and the casserole is heated all the way through.

Serve with fresh green salad and oven-toasted garlic bread. Leftovers can be reheated in microwave. But, most likely there won't be any.

Serves 4 – 6

Pepper Schwartz

Professor of Sociology at the University of Washington, Pepper Schwartz is a resident of Seattle, Washington. She holds a B.A. and an M.A. from Washington University in St. Louis, where she was a Woodrow Wilson Fellow, and an M.A. and PhD in Sociology from Yale University.

Dr. Schwartz is the author of 14 books, including: *The Great Sex Weekend, The Lifetime Love and Sex Quiz Book, Everything You Know About Love and Sex is Wrong, 201 Questions to Ask Your Kids / 201 Questions to Ask Your Parents* and *Ten Talks Parents Must Have With Their Children About Sex and Character* (with Dominic Cappello).

A regular member of the KIRO-TV (Seattle) news staff for twelve years, Dr. Schwartz appears regularly on national TV news and documentaries. She is the author of more than 40 scholarly articles and has served as a consultant to national organizations. Dr. Schwartz lectures on relationship topics, women's issues, parent and child issues, communication between men and women in intimate and work relationships, and maintaining personal and family well-being in today's world.

ABOUT THE RECIPE:

"For me, Thanksgiving is the central celebration of the year. I have a group of people who come year after year, and the tables line up and expand for however many people need a place to go. The number has varied from a low of about 15 to a high of 34. I have several dishes that have to be made. But there always has to be zesty, fruity wild rice. I make vats of this recipe so I can have some the rest of the week. Hence, the recipe is imprecise on proportions since most people will be making this for smaller dinner parties."

– Pepper Schwartz

Thanksgiving Wild Rice

Cook the rice 'til it reaches the desired firmness – I like it quite firm but not hard. I also like the natural wild rice that has to be soaked, drained, and soaked and drained again to clean it. But that's not necessary. Plenty of wild rice comes ready to be cooked.

While the rice is cooking, dice the following with large handfuls of each – if you are making a recipe for 12 or more people – less if it is a smaller number:

• Chopped and blanched almonds (buy slivers and chop them into halves)
• Diced pecans
• Diced dried prunes
• Fresh chopped peeled mangos and apples (small bits) (if you can't get fresh mango you can substitute dried and increase the apples a bit)

Mix the ingredients into the rice 15 minutes before serving. Should be yummy!

Peggy Sholly

A native of Baton Rouge, Louisiana and born into a large Italian American family, Peggy learned to love food and enjoy it as a social aspect of life. She began performing at a young age and developed a warm, witty, and indomitable personality that has served her well. An alumnus of LSU, she married in her early twenties and began to creatively develop her passion for cooking. A wife and mother of three, she worked in the corporate world and was heavily involved in a variety of community and public speaking activities.

When Peggy's daughters-in-law asked her to teach them to cook, she drew upon her range of culinary experiences on the flavor trail from New Orleans to West Texas to create her private collection of recipes and mealtime hints. Friends and family encouraged her to put her recipes in print for the benefit of all. When Peggy remarried she becoming a cookbook author and publisher. Friends and family encouraged her to put her recipes in print. Her cookbook, *Down Home Delicious: Spice Up your Life with Incredible Gulf Coast Cooking* is, like Peggy, full of passion and love and the kinds of dishes that make life worth living. She currently leads a hectic schedule of book signings, cooking classes, radio interviews and travel.

ABOUT THE RECIPE:

"Sweet Tater'umpkin Pie was born when my daughter requested I provide a recipe she could cook on a Thanksgiving TV segment along with her husband, a meteorologist. After she declined several suggestions, I finally asked what she liked and she said sweet potatoes. Because sweet potato tends to be dry, I added pumpkin, did a little experimenting with taste combinations and Sweet Tater'umpkin was born. It was an instant success and a new favorite."

– Peggy Sholly

Down-Home Delicious Sweet Tater'umpkin Pie

2 large sweet potatoes
1³/₄ sticks (1³/₄ cup) butter
8 oz. cream cheese
1 cups all-purpose white flour
1 cup white granulated sugar
2¹/₂ cups pecan pieces
1 (16-oz.) can pumpkin
2 (14-oz.) cans Eagle Brand® Sweetened Condensed Milk
1¹/₂ cups light brown sugar
1 tsp. cinnamon
¹/₂ tsp. salt
4 large eggs
¹/₂ cup old fashioned oats
1 cup powdered confectioner's sugar
1 tsp. vanilla
1 (16-oz.) container Cool Whip®
1 cup "angel hair" sweetened coconut
Caramel sauce (optional)

Move oven rack to middle position. Preheat oven to 350 degrees. Wash sweet potatoes and poke two holes on either side of each to keep it from bursting when cooking. For large potatoes, microwave 20 minutes. Turn potatoes over after 10 minutes, then finish microwaving. Scoop warm potato from skin; measure 1¹/₂ - 2 cups potato (discard the rest or enjoy eating while you are cooking).

CREAM CHEESE CRUST

3/4 stick butter, softened (not melted)

4 oz. softened cream cheese (reserve remaining cream cheese for topping)

1 1/2 cups all-purpose white flour

1 cup white granulated sugar (or half white/half light brown sugar)

1 cup pecan pieces

Generously grease a 9 x 13-inch decorative oven proof baking dish or 2 deep dish 9-inch pie plates. Combine ingredients and pat into bottom(s) of baking dish. Crust will be sticky but it's worth the effort. Cook 5 minutes in 350 degree oven. After crust has baked 5 minutes, remove from oven and set aside. Leave oven on while you prepare filling.

FILLING

1 1/2-2 cups sweet potatoes

1 (16-oz.) canned pumpkin

2 (14-oz.) cans Eagle Brand Condensed Milk

3/4 cup light brown sugar, packed

1/2 stick 1/4 cup) butter, melted

1/2 tsp. cinnamon

1/2 tsp. salt

4 large or jumbo eggs

Put all filling ingredients in a blender or food processor and blend well. Pour filling over crust(s), then return dish to oven and bake for 35-40 minutes for large pan or 25-30 for pie plates, at 350 degrees or until a knife inserted in center of filling comes out clean.

While filling is baking, make nut topping.

NUT TOPPING

1 1/2 cups coarsely chopped pecans

3/4 cup packed light brown sugar

1/2 cup old fashioned oats

1/2 teaspoon cinnamon

1/2 stick (1/4 cup) melted butter

Blend ingredients together. When filling is finished baking, remove pan(s) from oven just long enough to spread nut topping all over top. Move oven rack to next higher level and change oven temperature to 425 degrees. Return baking pan(s) to oven and bake another 5-10 minutes, until topping is brown and crisp. Remove pan(s) from oven and turn oven off.

Cool completely on a wire rack; when filling is thoroughly cooled (several hours), top with Cloud Topping. HINT: When pie is partially cooled but not hot, put wire rack on shelf in freezer (on top of frozen food is okay) and put pie there to speed up cooling. When thoroughly cooled, remove from refrigerator or freezer. While pie is cooling, make cloud topping.

CLOUD TOPPING
4 oz. cream cheese, softened
1 cup powdered confectioner's sugar
1 tsp. vanilla
1(16-oz.) container Cool Whip
1 cup sweetened angel flaked coconut – optional
Caramel sundae sauce – optional

In a large bowl, mix cream cheese, powdered sugar and vanilla until well blended; stir in Cool Whip. Spread topping on cooled filling. Sprinkle with coconut and drizzle caramel lightly over all. Refrigerate until ready to serve.

Serves 12 (Recipe can be cut in half)

Jennie Shortridge

Bestselling author Jennie Shortridge has three published novels. Her nonfiction work has appeared in a wide range of magazines and newspapers, including *Glamour*, *Mademoiselle*, *Natural Home* and others. She is a regular volunteer for 826 Seattle and makes her home in the Queen Anne neighborhood with her husband, Matt.

PUBLISHED WORKS:

Love and Biology at the Center of the Universe, Eating Heaven and *Riding with the Queen.*

ABOUT THE RECIPE:

"As anyone in his or her right mind knows, food is more than nourishment. Food can be love (in doses moderate enough not to kill you), especially when offered in that spirit. If my husband has a bad day, fried chicken and potatoes is the antidote. If I'm the one who needs a hug, he makes his mom's shepherd's pie that is comforting and warm. If we need a romance injection (as one sometimes does after 19 years of togetherness) we pull out the champagne and brie, the strawberries, and importantly, the dark chocolate. Here's my recipe for Barry White Baked Brie, a gooey treat so sensuous and sumptuous you might just fall in love all over again."

– Jennie Shortridge

Barry White Baked Brie

A hunk (a hunk) of burning brie. Well, not burning yet. Cold brie is
    best at this point.
1 sheet frozen ready-made puff pastry dough, such as Pepperidge
    Farm, brought to room temperature.
2 Tbsp. fig jam. If you hate figs, make it raspberry, or peach. Use
    something you like. You don't have to suffer for love.
1 Tbsp. crumbled and toasted nuts: pecans, walnuts, pistachios,
    hazelnuts. Again, something you like. And toasting is easy: just
    sprinkle them in a dry frying pan on medium heat, toss around a
    few times, and *voilá*.
A dribble of honey or maple syrup.
1 egg white

Spray a baking sheet with a light coat of healthy canola oil. Actually, make that
melted butter. Melt a puddle of butter in the middle of the baking sheet. Lay the
pastry sheet in the puddle. Place the brie in the middle of the sheet, then spoon on
jam and nuts, and drizzle with honey or syrup. Heck, you might as well throw some
butter in there, too.

Carefully fold the pastry sheet tightly around the brie, cutting away extra dough (save
that for snacking later, post romance) until you have a trim, solid wrapped brie. Use
egg white (or butter) to seal the edges and flip the brie over.

Brush with the remaining egg white and place the cookie sheet in a 375-degree oven
for 12 to 15 minutes.

When pastry turns golden, press against it to ensure the brie has softened. You
may want to poke with a knife. Don't worry about ruining its appearance. It's the
gooeyness that counts.

Serve with slices of apple and pear, baguette and crackers. Or, if you're in the mood,
dripping from fingers once it has cooled to the touch.

Karin Slaughter

Most authors believe in the adage "write what you know." But international-bestselling suspense writer Karin Slaughter believes in writing about what scares her most.

Her Grant County series is based on a collection of small towns she knew growing up in Georgia. She believes that it is a great place to find dastardly deeds. "Being a Southerner, I'm interested in sex, violence, religion and all the things that make life interesting. I remember being scared out of my wits as a young child."

"My dad believed in scaring us as we were growing up," she says. "Scaring the boys who wanted to date us, more. But it was something he believed in doing. So, he told us all these really scary stories. Some of them true; some, maybe not. I think we turned out all right because of it." A long-time resident of Atlanta, she splits her time between the kitchen and the living room.

PUBLISHED WORKS:

The Will Trent/Atlanta series includes *Triptych,* and *Fractured.* The Grant County series includes *Blindsighted, Kisscut, A Faint Cold Fear, Indelible, Faithless* and *Beyond Reach.*

ABOUT THE RECIPE:

"Cathy's Coke Roast was mentioned in my third book, *A Faint Cold Fear*. I was shocked by the number of people who wrote in and asked me for the recipe, mostly because in the South, we do a lot of cooking with Coke, and this is a very old recipe that just about everyone down here watched their grandmother use. I made a little movie about it and put it on my website. It's been years now, but it's still one of the most popular pages folks visit when they go to the site!" (www.karinslaughter.com)

– Karin Slaughter

Cathy's Coke® Roast

1 liter of Coke®
1 rump roast
Bay leaves
Low-sodium beef broth
Chopped carrots, celery, potatoes, Vidalia onions and mushrooms

Put roast in large bowl, cover with Coke. Add 2 bay leaves and refrigerate overnight, covered. Drain Coke and put roast in slow cooker. Add chopped vegetables to slow cooker. Add spices as desired. Pour beef broth to fill halfway. Cook on high for 3 hours. Cook on low for 3 hours. Best served with biscuits. Yum!

Serves 4 - 8

Garth Stein

Filmmaker and author of three novels, Garth Stein has released *How Evan Broke His Head and Other Secrets*, winner of a Pacific Northwest Booksellers Association Book Award, *Raven Stole the Moon* and *The Art of Racing in the Rain*. He also has written a full-length play, "Brother Jones," which received its first production in Los Angeles, and was described as "brimming with intensity" by *L.A. Weekly*.

After receiving his M.F.A. in Film from Columbia University in 1990, Garth worked as a documentary filmmaker for several years, co-producing "The Last Party," a documentary feature starring Robert Downey, Jr., and "The Lunch Date," which won an Academy Award for Live Action Short. He has directed and/or produced several award-winning films, including a chronicle of his sister's brain surgery for epilepsy, "When Your Head's Not a Head, It's a Nut," which aired nationally on PBS and in Japan.

Born in Los Angeles and raised in Seattle, Garth's ancestry is diverse: his mother, a native of Alaska, is of Tlingit Indian and Irish descent. His father, a Brooklyn native, is the child of Jewish emigrants from Austria. After spending his childhood in Seattle and then living in New York City, Garth returned to Seattle, where he currently lives with his family and his dog, Comet.

ABOUT THE RECIPE:

"This recipe evolved from a simple cannellini bean and garlic side dish I used to make for my wife when we were first married. Later, I added more stock, Parmesan and some escarole, and it became a soup. And finally, I got to this form after I saw someone cook clams and sausages together on TV – I didn't know that was possible! I find it works great with my family, as my kids won't eat certain things or will only eat one thing if it hasn't touched something else. With this soup, I can pull out sausage for one kid, some clams for the other. I can leave out the chili pepper for my wife or add extra pepper when my father-in-law is in town. The trick with this dish: make more than you think you need, because everyone loves it!"

– Garth Stein

Clams with Sausage, Beans and Pasta

Olive oil
$^2/_3$ lb. Italian sausage
4-6 cloves of garlic, sliced
2 lbs. Manila clams (the little ones)
$^1/_2$ cup white wine
3 cups – or more – of chicken stock
2 cups of cooked pasta
1 can cannellini or Great Northern beans, drained
$^1/_2$ tsp. – or more – crushed red pepper
$^1/_2$ cup grated Parmesan cheese
A small handful of chopped, fresh Italian parsley

1. Cook 1 lb. of shells or orecheitte or whatever pasta holds broth well (not spaghetti). Reserve about two cups for this dish. The rest you can feed to the kids with butter and olive oil.

2. Heat a couple of tablespoons of olive oil in a deep sauce pan, and cook up about a pound of sweet Italian sausage, removed from its casing and crumbled, until it is well browned. Skim off about a third of it to give to the kids. Keep the rest in the pan.

3. Add the clams and the wine. Cover. Cook two or three minutes until the clams have opened. Take a scoopful of the clam/sausage mixture and save it for your son who likes clams with sausages.

4. Add 2$^1/_2$ or 3 cups of chicken stock. Add the beans. Add the two cups of pasta you saved. Add more broth if you think you need it. (If you *think* you need it, you probably do!) Let it simmer for a couple of minutes.

5. Add the Parmesan cheese. If you're into heat, add up to 1 tsp. crushed red pepper flakes, keeping in mind that 1 tsp. will give you four stars on the five star scale. Try ½ tsp. the first time you make this.

6. After it's simmered for a few more minutes and looks like it tastes really good, add about a handful of chopped Italian parsley, stir, and remove from heat.

7. Serve in bowls. This amount should serve four hungry people pretty well. Plus two kids eating only pasta, one kid eating pasta and sausage, and one kid eating pasta, sausage, and clams.

8. My family likes this served with a nice, crunchy baguette and a salad of romaine, sweet onions, and quartered tomatoes dressed with white wine vinegar and olive oil. Except one of my kids, who will only eat strawberries or honey dew melon. And the other, who only eats red bell peppers.

9. Everybody is now happy, and they are very impressed with your cooking. But they still won't help with the dishes!

Rick Steves

Travel author, Rick Steves, grew up in Edmonds, Washington and studied at the University of Washington where he received degrees in Business Administration and European History. But his real education came in Europe. Each year since 1972, he spends 120 days a year in Europe. Devoting one-third of his adult life living out of a suitcase in Europe has shaped his thinking. Today, he employs 80 people at his Europe Through the Back Door headquarters in Edmonds where he produces 30 guidebooks on European travel, the most popular travel series in America on public television. In addition, he stars in a weekly hour-long national public radio show and writes a weekly syndicated column. Rick and his wife, Anne, have traveled for the last 18 years with their two kids, Andy and Jackie.

PUBLISHED WORKS:

Europe 101: History & Art for the Traveler, Rick Steves' European Christmas Book, Mona Winks and *Europe Through the Back Door* plus more than 24 guidebooks for various European countries and cities in addition to phrasebooks and dictionaries in French, Spanish and German.

ABOUT THE RECIPE:

"Early in my career, I taught Budget European Travel Classes through the Experimental College at the University of Washington. It was in one of these classes in 1983 that I met Anne, my future wife. We had time for one date before I left for four months of working in Europe. Tour members would courier these Cowboy Cookies and love letters in simple shoeboxes over to me. Back to her would come my travel yarns, overflowing on postcards. For more than 24 years, it's been my favorite thing she makes for me."

– Rick Steves

Cowboy Cookies

2 cups flour
1 tsp. soda
½ tsp. salt
½ tsp. baking powder
Sift these four ingredients together and set aside.

1 cup butter
1 cup granulated sugar
1 cup brown sugar
2 eggs
2 cups oatmeal
1 tsp. vanilla
1 12-oz. package semi-sweet chocolate chips

1. Blend butter and sugars well. Add eggs and beat until light.

2. Add flour mixture and mix well.

3. Add oats, vanilla and chocolate chips.

4. Drop cookie dough onto a greased cookie sheet.

5. Bake at 350 degrees for 12 to 15 minutes.

Nanci Tangeman

Nancy Tangeman has lived abroad in the United Kingdom, Uzbekistan and the Netherlands. That may be the reason for her bestselling book, *40 Excuses to Get Together with the Girls*, a guide for women who want to try new things and spend more time with their female friends. She and her husband are the founders of MAD Grants, a grant program in the Highline, Washington and Portland, Oregon school districts. Her website is www.nancitangeman.com.

ABOUT THE RECIPE:

"In 1997, business took my husband and me to Tashkent, Uzbekistan for two years. While we lived there, I published an English-language cultural newspaper, covering a culinary scene where matching cutlery and steady supplies of anything were rare. However, there were some wonderful surprises: the secret pork chop restaurant (in the mostly Muslim country) and our favorite Georgian café. Every few months the owners would drive to Tbilisi to pick up a fresh supply of Georgian wine. They'd return with their aging Lada auto crammed with 2-liter soda bottles full of some of the best red wine I've ever tasted. They'd fill our own recycled bottles for around

25 cents apiece. My favorite dishes at their restaurant were carrots with a nut paste center and Khachapuri. Having tried to artistically stuff nut paste into carrots, I think it's best that I share this Khachapuri recipe, instead."

– Nanci Tangeman

Khachapuri
(Georgian Cheese Bread)

¾ cup milk
1½ packages (4½ tsp.) active dry yeast
½ tsp. honey
6 Tbsp. (¾ stick) butter, at room temperature
¼ tsp. ground coriander seed
1¾ tsp. salt
2 cups unbleached white flour
1 lb. Muenster cheese
½ lb. pot cheese
3 eggs
1 Tbsp. melted butter

Heat the milk to lukewarm (105 degrees). Dissolve the yeast and honey in ¼ cup of the milk. Set aside to proof for 10 minutes, then stir in the remaining milk. Add the room temperature butter, ground coriander seed, 1½ teaspoons of the salt, and the flour, mixing well.

Turn the dough onto a floured board and knead until smooth and elastic, about 10 minutes. Place in a greased bowl, turning the dough to grease the top. Cover and allow to rise in a warm place until doubled in bulk, 1½ to 2 hours.

To prepare the filling, grate the Muenster cheese. In a medium bowl, with a wooden spoon, cream the pot cheese. Stir in the grated Muenster until well blended. Beat the eggs and stir into the cheese mixture along with the remaining ¼ teaspoon of salt. Beat until smooth and light. Set aside.

When the dough has doubled in bulk, punch it down and then let rise again until doubled, about 45 minutes. Punch down and divide into three equal pieces.

On a floured board, roll each piece of dough into a circle about 12 inches in diameter. Grease three 8-inch cake or pie pans. Center a round of dough in each pan.

Divide the cheese mixture into three equal parts. Place a third of the filling on each circle of dough, heaping it in the center. Then begin folding the edges of the dough in, toward the center, moving in a clockwise direction, allowing each fold of dough to overlap the previous one, until the cheese mixture is completely enclosed in the pleated dough. Grasp the excess dough in the center of the bread and twist it into a topknot to seal.

Preheat the oven to 375 degrees.

Let the breads stand for 10 minutes, then brush with the melted butter. Bake for about 45 minutes, or until browned. Slip the *Khachapuri* out of the pans and serve hot or at room temperature. Cut into wedges to serve.

Serves 8 – 12

Patrick Taylor

Photo by Dorothy Tinman

Born in 1941, Patrick Taylor was brought up in Bangor, Northern Ireland, and received his medical education in Ulster. He initially practiced in a rural village akin to *Ballybucklebo* before taking specialist training in Obstetrics and Gynecology. After living in Belfast through the first two years of the Irish Troubles (1969-1994), he and his family immigrated to Canada where he pursued a career in medical research and teaching in the field of human infertility. His contributions have been honored with three lifetime achievement awards including the Lifetime Award of Excellence of the Canadian Fertility and Andrology Society. Taylor, an Ulsterman who spent 37 years in Canada, now lives in his native Ireland. He is a distinguished medical research worker, author, off-shore sailor, model boat-builder and father of two grown-up children.

PUBLISHED WORKS:

An Irish Country Village, An Irish Country Doctor, Now and in the Hour of Our Death, The Apprenticeship of Dr. Laverty, Pray for Us Sinners and *Only Wounded: Ulster Stories.*

ABOUT THE RECIPE:

"If I tried to boil an egg, I'd burn the water. But, I knew a woman who cooked like an angel. I was a junior doctor in training, moonlighting for rural GPs.

The housekeeper to one, and she was also a *seannchie*, a story teller, who became the model for Mrs. Kinky Kinkaid, my fictional housekeeper. In the 1960s, I recorded her stories. I also recorded many of her traditional Irish recipes that appear at the end of all my *Irish Country* books. Here are two of hers. One is for Colcannon, an Irish potato dish properly eaten on the Sunday closest to the First of August and made from that year's first-pulled new potatoes. The other recipe is for proper Leek and Potato soup."

– Patrick Taylor

Colcannon

675 gr. (1½ lbs.) or 3 cups of mashed potatoes, still hot
225gr. (8 oz.) or 1 cup Savoy cabbage, cooked and chopped
125 ml. (4 oz.) or ½ cup cream
125 ml (4 oz.) or ½ cup milk
Small bunch spring onions chopped
55 gr. (2 oz.) ¼ cup butter

Combine the potato and cabbage in a serving bowl. Cook the chopped spring onions in the milk until soft. Add the cream and seasonings. Mix into the hot potato mixture. Dot with butter and serve.

Serves 3 – 4

Leek and Potato Soup

1 chopped onion
3 leeks
4 potatoes
Knob of butter
Vegetable stock
10 oz. (1¼ cups) cream
Salt and pepper
A little parsley to garnish

Fry the onion gently for about 10 minutes until cooked but still transparent. Add the well washed, trimmed and chopped leeks. Cook for another 5 minutes. Then add the chopped potatoes and add enough vegetable stock to cover. Season and cook for about 20 minutes until potatoes are cooked.

Adriana Trigiani

Beloved by millions of readers around the world for her hilarious and heartwarming novels, Adriana Trigiani was raised in a small coal-mining town in southwest Virginia. She chose her hometown for the setting of her debut novel, the critically acclaimed and bestselling *Big Stone Gap*. It was followed by the sequels *Big Cherry Holler*, *Milk Glass Moon*, and *Home to Big Stone Gap*. Since 1999, Adriana has delivered a novel each year to her devoted fans. *The Queen of the Big Time*, *Rococo* and *Lucia, Lucia* were all instant *New York Times* bestsellers. She also teamed up with her family for *Cooking with My Sisters*, co-authored by her sister, Mary, with contributions from their sisters and mom. The cookbook-memoir features recipes and stories dating back a hundred years from both sides of their Italian-American family.

Adriana has written the screenplay and will direct the movie adaptation of her novel, *Big Stone Gap*. Coming soon: *Bella Rosa*, *Very Valentine* and *The Viola Chesterton Chronicles* (a novel for young adults).

ABOUT THE RECIPE:

"The Aunt Irma sponge cake is an Italian American classic recipe. The basis of many of our fancy desserts is a sponge cake, even though we've been known to serve it plain with a cup of good coffee. There are lots of alternatives to dress this cake up! It can be smothered in homemade jam or dusted with powdered sugar or made into a mean layer in your tiramisu. Your call. We love it a variety of ways – the always-scrumptious, ever-reliable sponge cake."

– Adriana Trigiani

Zia Irma's Italian Sponge Cake

1 cup cake flour
6 eggs, separated
1 cup of sugar
½ tsp. salt
½ tsp. cream of tartar
¼ tsp. almond flavoring
¼ cup water
10 inch un-greased tube pan

Preheat the oven 325 degrees.

Sift 1 cup of the cake flour.

Beat egg yolk until lemon colored. Gradually add 1 cup of sugar. Alternate the flour and ¼ tsp. almond flavoring in ¼ cup of water to egg yolk mixture at low speed.

In a separate bowl, beat egg whites until frothy and they stand in peaks. Fold egg yolk mixture into whites just until blended.

Pour batter into 10-inch, un-greased tube pan.

Bake for one hour at 325 degrees or until the cake springs back when lightly touched in center.

Let sit in inverted position until cool.

Elaine Viets

As a young girl, Elaine Viets was taught the virtues of South St. Louis: the importance of hard work, housecleaning, and paying cash. She managed to forget almost everything she learned, which is why she turned to mystery writing.

Living in South Florida has not improved her character. But it has given her the bestselling *Dead-End Job* series. Like her amateur detective, Helen Hawthorne, Elaine actually works those rotten jobs. Perhaps her early training has given her a lifelong fascination with under-employment. She and Helen both know working for a living can be murder.

Elaine has served on the national boards of the Mystery Writers of America and Sisters in Crime. She lives in Fort Lauderdale, Florida, with her husband, actor Don Crinklaw, where they collect speeding tickets.

PUBLISHED WORKS:

Clubbed to Death, Accessory to Murder, Murder with Reservations, High Heels Are Murder, Murder Unleashed, Dying in Style, Just Murdered and *Dying to Call You.*

ABOUT THE RECIPE:

"My husband Don's idea of a balanced diet is a 12-ounce steak and a six-ounce baked potato. Fiber is something from "CSI." Omega-3 oils belong in a Buick. Vegetables and fruit are found in drinks – cocktail onions, olives, cherries and lemons. He nearly punched the bartender who slipped a tiny Brussels sprout into his drink. He thought it was an abomination. Don, however, does get lots of legumes. He likes salted bar peanuts.

I figured there was no point in lecturing Don on healthy eating. I'd simply have to show him the right way to eat. What was the point if I lived forever but was all alone? I'd be spending my declining years being hit on by geezers in Fort Lauderdale. Since I have all my teeth, I am a hot babe in Florida.

Instead, I made him a fruit smoothie. I'd gotten the recipe at a Canyon Ranch lecture and sort of tweaked it. Don acted like I was smuggling in something illegal when I brought home soymilk and ground flaxseed.

I gave him a taste of the first smoothie. "Not bad," he said. "But it needs vodka."

I didn't answer him with statistics on the joys of healthy food. Instead, I started making a smoothie every day around 11 a.m. Soon Don was hanging around the kitchen whenever he heard the blender, like a cat that rushes in when we turn on the can opener. "Got any extra?" he asked.

His morning smoothie has become a ritual. Don's barber even said Don's hair seemed to be coming in thicker after a few months of drinking the smoothies.

I make no such claim. I never mention it's full of flaxseed and soymilk and Don manages to overlook its healthy properties. Now I can't wait for him to try my whole-wheat martini."

– Elaine Viets

Don't-Tell-Anyone-It's-Healthy Fruit Smoothie

1 cup vanilla flavored soy milk
2 cups fresh or frozen strawberries, blueberries, bananas, peaches or
    other fruit. (I use frozen blueberries, a frozen banana, and fresh or
    defrosted frozen strawberries.)
1 Tbsp. ground flaxseed (available at health food stores)
1 scoop of protein powder
Cinnamon to taste (I like a lot and sprinkle some on each layer,
    especially the protein powder layer.)

Whip fruit, soymilk, etc., in a blender until smooth. Use a blender with a good motor, and add the milk first, or the blender will burn out. I run it twice on the "ice crush" setting and twice on the "smoothie" setting.

This is a recipe you can adjust to your tastes. I like it with more strawberries. Don prefers extra blueberries. If you like a thicker milkshake consistency, add a cup of ice cubes.

Serves about four cups

Susan Vreeland

Recognized internationally for her historical fiction on art themes, Susan Vreeland is a artistic sensation. Her newest *New York Times* bestseller, *Luncheon of the Boating Party*, reveals Renoir's masterpiece and the personalities involved in its making who reflect the vibrancy of late nineteenth century Paris. Her story collection, *Life Studies*, reveals Impressionist and Post-Impressionist painters, and shows ordinary people having profound encounters with art. *The Forest Lover* follows the rebel Canadian painter, Emily Carr, into the British Columbia wilderness. *The Passion of Artemisia* illuminates the Italian Baroque painter, Artemisia Gentileschi, one of the first women to make her living solely by her brush. *Girl in Hyacinth Blue* traces an alleged Vermeer painting through the centuries. Vreeland's novels have been translated into 25 languages and her short fiction has appeared in many publications.

ABOUT THE RECIPE:

"I am happy to contribute a period French recipe for an item served at one of the luncheons in my novel, *Luncheon of the Boating Party*. The book takes its title from Renoir's painting of the same name, which shows 14 people around a dining table on the terrace of a restaurant overlooking the Seine. The painting truly unites cuisine and art and literature. *Bon appetit!"*

— *Susan Vreeland*

Poires Belle Hélène

For the pears:
6 firm pears
¾ cup sugar
3 cups water
1 vanilla bean
2 lemons

For the chocolate sauce:
8 oz. semi-sweet chocolate, chopped
½ cup water
1 Tbsp. brandy

Peel a pear, leaving stem intact and rub immediately with a cut half of a lemon. Working from the bottom, scoop out the seeds and membrane using a vegetable peeler. Repeat with the remaining pears. Pare the peel from the other lemon and squeeze out the juice, reserving the peel and juice.

Cut the vanilla bean in half. Combine the water, vanilla bean, lemon peel, lemon juice and sugar in a saucepan. Heat until the sugar has dissolved, then bring to a boil.

Remove the pan from the heat; add the whole pears. Cut a piece of parchment paper (wax paper will do) the same diameter as the saucepan. Dampen it and place on top of the pears to keep them submerged while poaching. Simmer the pears over low heat until tender, about 24-35 minutes, depending on the ripeness. Let the pears cool in the poaching liquid.

Combine the water and chocolate in a saucepan and melt over low heat until smooth. Remove from heat and stir in the brandy. Keep the sauce warm.

Drain the pears well and place one in the center of each of six chilled serving plates. Arrange small scoops of ice cream around the pears. Gently spoon the chocolate sauce over the pears and serve. Pass remaining chocolate sauce.

Serves 6

Kathleen Walls

Kathleen Walls is the creator of *Georgia's Ghostly Getaways* based on the last colony's turbulent history as a natural breeding round for ghost stories and legends. From Revolutionary soldiers to Confederate officers, from southern belles to wicked witches, from spirit cats to howling prehistoric dogs, Georgia has some of the most unique ghosts anywhere. Combine that with warm climate, Victorian and Antebellum mansions and you have a guide to adventure. She has also written *Finding Florida's Phantoms*, *Last Step*, *Kudzu* and several other titles.

A successful travel writer and photographer who has been published in numerous magazines and journals, she currently publishes her own online travel magazine, *American Roads* (www.americanroads.net).

ABOUT THE RECIPE:

"When I first moved to the Sunshine State from New Orleans, I was amazed at the prolific groves of citrus and other subtropical fruit. This was back before Disney arrived in Florida and anyone who loved to wander through the wild lands along the rivers and lakes came in contact with many wild versions of oranges, tangerines, grapefruit and mangos. If you ever go exploring in Florida, you may even discover a wild mango tree of your own. Either way, you can always whip up a batch of my mango salsa!"

– Kathleen Walls

Mango Salsa

1 large just-ripe mango (you can use canned if you can't get fresh ones)
1 medium jalapeno pepper
½ medium onion
1 small bell pepper
1 Tbsp. lime juice

Chop the first four ingredients coarsely and mix well. Add the lime juice over the fruits. Let the mixture sit in refrigerator for at least an hour for the flavors to mix. Stir in a generous helping of Southern hospitality and you have a sure-fire recipe for ghost-hunting travel, Southern style.

Serve with sour cream, as a dip for your favorite chips.

Serves 3 – 4

Alice Waters

Renowned chef, author, and owner of Chez Panisse in Berkeley, California, Alice Waters pioneered a culinary philosophy based on using only the freshest local, organic products, picked in season. Chez Panisse was named best restaurant in the country by *Gourmet Magazine*. In 1995, Alice founded The Edible Schoolyard, a one-acre garden and kitchen classroom that incorporates her ideas about food and culture into the public school curriculum. The School Lunch Initiative, a landmark agreement between the Berkeley Unified School District and the Chez Panisse Foundation, will be responsible for the district-wide expansion of this project, with the goal of bringing children into a new relationship to food. Alice is also vice president of Slow Food International, a non-profit organization that promotes and celebrates local, artisanal food traditions, with members in over 100 countries.

PUBLISHED WORKS:

Chez Panisse Café Cookbook, The Art of Simple Food: Notes, Lessons, and Recipes from a Delicious Revolution, Chez Panisse Vegetables, Chez Panisse Fruit and *Chez Panisse Menu Cookbook.*

ABOUT THE RECIPE:

"A good, tasty use for a variety of vegetables is vinegar pickles. Unlike fermented pickles, that take weeks or months, these are ready to eat in a few minutes and will keep for a week. These pickles can be used in a variety of ways and are good to have on hand to brighten up a charcuterie plate – or as an hors d'oeuvre on their own. Feel free to alter the ingredients of the brine: try using red instead of white vinegar or adding saffron or other kinds of dried chiles or fresh slices of jalapeño."

– Alice Waters

Fresh-Pickled Vegetables

1½ cups white-wine vinegar
1¾ cups water
2½ Tbsp. sugar
½ bay leaf
4 thyme sprigs
Half of a dried cayenne pepper or a pinch of dried chile flakes
½ tsp. coriander seeds
2 whole cloves
1 garlic clove, peeled and cut in half
A big pinch of salt

Prepare the pickling solution by combining all the ingredients listed and bringing them to a boil. Cook each type of vegetable separately in this boiling brine, scooping them out when cooked but still a little bit crisp. Set them aside to cool. Once all the vegetables are cooked and cooled and the pickling solution has cooled to room temperature, combine the vegetables, transfer to jars or another covered container, cover with the pickle brine and refrigerate.

Use this method to pickle little florets of cauliflower, sliced carrots, quartered pearl or cipolline onions, halved okra pods, small turnips cut in to wedges with some their stems still attached, whole green beans, small cubes of celery root, and more. Sometimes I just slice red onions very thin and pour the boiling brine over them. By the time they cool, they will have cooked just enough. They are delicious served with smoked fish and new potatoes.

Debra Webb

Writing her first story at age nine and her first romance at 13, Debra Webb launched an early career. It wasn't until she spent three years working for the military behind the Iron Curtain and within the confining political walls of Berlin, Germany, that she realized her true calling. A five-year stint with NASA on the Space Shuttle Program reinforced her love of the endless possibilities within her grasp as a storyteller. A collision course between suspense and romance was set. Debra and her family live in Atlanta, where she writes bestselling spine-tingling romance suspense and action packed romantic thrillers.

PUBLISHED WORKS:

Faceless, Nameless, Traceless, Safe By His Side, The Bodyguard's Baby, Longwalker's Child, Protective Custody, Special Assignment: Baby, Solitary Soldier and *Personal Protector.*

ABOUT THE RECIPE:

"This recipe was given to me by a very dear friend, Mike (Maureen) Cooper. I was running late for a meeting one night and Mike was kind enough to share her dinner with me. The soup was the best I'd ever eaten. I grew up on a potato farm, so I'm pretty picky about potatoes prepared in any fashion. If you're a lover of potatoes, you will be thrilled with this recipe."

– Debra Webb

Miss Jean's Potato Soup

1 quart vegetable stock
1 can cream of celery soup
1 large can baked potato soup with cheddar cheese & bacon
1 jar real bacon bits
1 bag hash browns
Salt and pepper to taste
1 bag baby spinach leaves

While the vegetable stock is warming, brown the hash brown potatoes per package directions. Drain well and mix all ingredients except spinach – add it just before you serve so it doesn't become over-cooked.

Tips: If you like it "soupier," add more water. Scallions or sharp cheddar cheese make a good garnish. The browner the hash browns are, the more they stay together. Less browning and you have a thicker, creamier soup with fewer chunks. The spinach is optional – but it does work in a green veggie.

Serves 4 – 6

Susan Wiggs

Susan Wiggs' life is all about family, friends, fiction...and sometimes even food. Some of her novels even feature her favorite recipes. She lives at the water's edge on Bainbridge Island, Washington and she commutes to her writers' group in a 17-foot motorboat. She's been featured on NPR's "Talk of the Nation," and is a popular speaker.

According to *Publishers Weekly*, Wiggs writes with "refreshingly honest emotion," and the *Salem Statesman Journal* adds that she is "one of our best observers of stories of the heart [who] knows how to capture emotion on virtually every page of every book." Booklist characterizes her books as "real and true and unforgettable." She is the recipient of three RITA Awards from Romace Writers of America and four-starred reviews from *Publishers Weekly*. Several of her books have been listed as top Booksense picks and optioned as feature films. Her novels have been translated into more than two dozen languages and have made national bestseller lists, including *USA Today*, *Washington Post* and *The New York Times*.

The author is a former teacher, a Harvard graduate, an avid hiker, an amateur photographer, a good skier and terrible golfer, yet her favorite form of exercise is curling up with a good book. Readers can learn more at www.susanwiggs.com.

PUBLISHED WORKS:

Irish Magic, Just Breathe, Summer by the Sea, The You I Never Knew, Passing Through Paradise, That Summer Place, The Horsemaster's Daughter and *The Charm School.*

ABOUT THE RECIPE:

"Each year on Bainbridge Island, Washington, on the Fourth of July, there's a potluck brunch before the parade. It's our unofficial welcome for summer. I try to bring something different every year, but this one gets requested over and over again. It's moist and has an intriguing mingling of flavors. Everyone in the Pacific Northwest grows rosemary because the deer leave it alone. Also, this cake is very forgiving and easy to make. This recipe is semi-original, adapted from something I saw on the Food Network a long time ago."

– Susan Wiggs

Rosemary Olive Oil Cake

3 eggs
2 cups sugar
1½ cups extra-virgin olive oil
1½ cups milk
¼ cup triple sec, Cointreau or Grand Marnier
¼ cup frozen orange juice concentrate
3 tsp. lemon zest
2 cups flour
½ tsp. baking soda
½ tsp. baking powder
1 tsp. salt
1-2 tsp. chopped fresh rosemary
½ cup orange or lemon marmalade
Rosemary sprigs and powdered sugar, for garnish

Preheat the oven to 350 degrees. Oil and flour a Bundt® pan.

Beat the eggs, sugar, olive oil, milk, liqueur, orange juice, and lemon zest. Add the dry ingredients, including 1-2 teaspoons chopped fresh rosemary, and beat well. Pour into Bundt pan. Bake for 50 minutes to 1 hour, until it tests done. Place on a rack to cool. Run a knife around the edges and invert on a plate.

Warm the marmalade in the microwave and drizzle over the cake. Garnish with rosemary sprigs, sprinkle with powdered sugar.

Art Wolfe

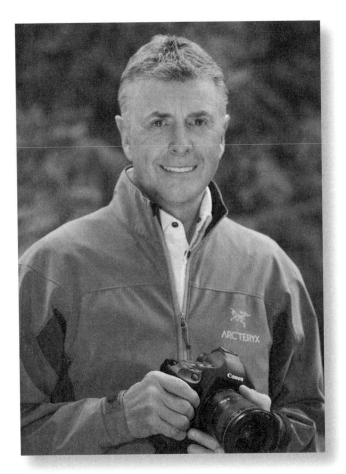

The son of commercial artists, Art Wolfe was born in Seattle and still calls the city home. He graduated from the University of Washington with degrees in fine arts and art education.

Over his 30-year career, the photographer, author and filmmaker has worked on every continent and in hundreds of locations. His stunning images interpret the world's fast-disappearing wildlife, landscapes and native cultures. Art's photographs are recognized throughout the world for their mastery of color, composition and perspective.

Art Wolfe has taken an estimated one million images in his lifetime and has released more than sixty books, including the award-winning *Vanishing Act*, *The High Himalaya*, *Water: Worlds between Heaven & Earth*, *Tribes*, *Rainforests of the World*, *The Art of Photographing Nature* as well as children's titles. *Graphis* included his books *Light on the Land* and *Migrations* on its list of the 100 best books published in the 1990s.

He published the award-winning *Africa* and *Edge of the Earth – Corner of the Sky*, which captured several publishing awards. He has been awarded with a coveted Alfred Eisenstaedt Magazine Photography Award as well as named Outstanding

Nature Photographer of the Year by the North American Nature Photography Association. The National Audubon Society recognized his work with its first Rachel Carson Award.

Art Wolfe has ventured into the world of television production with "On Location with Art Wolfe," "Techniques of the Masters" and as host of "American Photo's Safari." He made his public television debut with "Travels to the Edge with Art Wolfe," an intimate and upbeat series that offers insights on nature, culture and digital photography.

ABOUT THE RECIPE:

"One of my photo editors taught me this recipe many years ago and it remains one of the easiest and favorite dishes to prepare. I like the nutty flavor of the whole-wheat pasta combined with the toasted pine nuts. The garlic, arugula and chili give it a nice bite. And, the Italian Asiago cheese adds a bit of sharp richness."

– *Art Wolfe*

Arugula and Asiago Pasta

8 Tbsp. olive oil
1 red chilli, chopped
3 cloves of garlic, chopped
2 cups of fresh arugula (washed and rinsed)
10 oz. whole-wheat spaghetti
Salt and freshly ground black pepper to taste
1 cup pine nuts (toasted)
1½ cup of shredded Italian Asiago cheese (Asiago d'allevo – the flavor
    is reminiscent of sharp Cheddar and Parmesan)

1. Cook the pasta to tender according to the packet instructions.

2. Heat the olive oil in a large, open pan; sauté the chilli and garlic for two minutes.

3. Add the arugula and stir through.

4. Drain the pasta and add to the pan.

5. Season with salt and pepper; add toasted pine nuts and toss together.

6. Transfer to serving bowl and liberally sprinkle the shredded Asiago cheese over the pasta.

Serves 3-4

The ablest writer is only a gardener first, and then a cook: his tasks are, carefully to select and cultivate his strongest and most nutritive thoughts; and when they are ripe, to dress them, wholesomely, and yet so that they may have a relish.

– Augustus William Hare (1792-1834)
and Julius Charles Hare (1795-1855),
Guesses at Truth, by Two Brothers (1827)